MVP
MOST VALUABLE PLAYER

Tony Óg Regan is one of Ireland's leading high-performance coaches, having worked with multiple All-Ireland winning teams. His experiences come from being a Galway senior hurler for more than ten years, upskilling himself in leadership, executive and performance psychology coaching, and working with high-performing teams at elite level over the past ten years, including the Tipperary hurling team (Munster and All-Ireland champions in 2016), the Limerick hurlers in 2019 and Ballygunner, All-Ireland club champions 2022.

He is passionate about helping organisations, individuals and teams develop their optimal mindset to be healthy, motivated and consistent performers in their personal and professional lives.

MVP
MOST VALUABLE PLAYER

RAISE YOUR GAME
UNLOCK YOUR POTENTIAL

TONY ÓG REGAN

HACHETTE
BOOKS
IRELAND

Copyright © 2025 Tony Óg Regan

The right of Tony Óg Regan to be identified as the author of the work has been asserted by him in accordance with the Copyright, Designs and Patents Act 1988.

First published in Ireland in 2025 by HACHETTE BOOKS IRELAND

1

All rights reserved. No part of this publication may be reproduced, stored in a retrieval system, or transmitted, in any form or by any means without the prior written permission of the publisher, nor be otherwise circulated in any form of binding or cover other than that in which it is published and without a similar condition being imposed on the subsequent purchaser.

Cataloguing in Publication Data is available from the British Library

ISBN 9781399732765

The Polyvagal chart is used with kind permission from Ruby Jo Walker, swtraumatraining.com.

Typeset in Garamond Premier Pro by Bookends Publishing Services, Dublin
Printed and bound in Great Britain by Clays Ltd, Elcograf S.p.A.

Hachette Books Ireland policy is to use papers that are natural, renewable and recyclable products and made from wood grown in sustainable forests. The logging and manufacturing processes are expected to conform to the environmental regulations of the country of origin.

Hachette Books Ireland
8 Castlecourt Centre
Castleknock
Dublin 15, Ireland

A division of Hachette UK Ltd
Carmelite House, 50 Victoria Embankment, London EC4Y 0DZ

www.hachettebooksireland.ie

I dedicate this book to my wife, kids, family and friends who have helped shape me into the person I am today. Thank you to all the people who back me and continue to give me opportunities in life. Keep showing up for each other.

In memory of the great people who have passed and were truly special people to have met: my grandparents, Uncle David, John Kearns, Gerry Kenneally, Andrew Rodgers and Niall Donohue.

CONTENTS

Introduction *ix*

1 Confusion versus Clarity *1*
2 Fear versus Courage *35*
3 Outcome versus Process *61*
4 Threat versus Challenge *89*
5 Panic versus Composure *119*
6 Doubt versus Confidence *141*
7 Pessimism versus Optimism *165*
8 Intensity versus Recovery *203*
9 Frazzled versus Flow *227*
10 Resistance versus Acceptance *245*

Conclusion *269*
Acknowledgements *277*
Bibliography *281*

Some names and identifying details have been changed throughout this book.

INTRODUCTION

I AM TONY ÓG REGAN. I WAS BORN IN UNIVERSITY Hospital Galway on 14 November 1983 and grew up in a small rural townland called Boleybeg in Rahoon on the outskirts of Galway city.

I spent a huge amount of my childhood playing and watching sport. Our front lawn was a hive of activity during the evenings and summer holidays. We would play soccer tournaments against our neighbouring townland, Tonabrucky, who featured the famous Kellys, Joyces and Kynes! These games happened almost weekly and were very competitive. When Wimbledon was on, we would put a tennis net up and play tennis for hours. We had a basketball hoop at the side of the house that would be used as target practice for hurling, Gaelic football and basketball.

Dad, who was known as 'Horse', was an inter-county footballer with Roscommon and went on to be director of sport in University College Galway for forty years. Mum has multiple All-Ireland medals in badminton, as she likes to remind us. My parents were very involved in our community. I remember Dad coaching multiple teams that my sisters and I played on in hurling, camogie and Gaelic football. My parents were always involved in school, charity and club activities, giving up their free time to help others in so many ways.

Through Dad's extensive involvement in coaching, we always had lots of sports equipment in our garage, be it cones, hurdles, ladders, poles or balls. We would regularly build obstacle courses with the neighbours and have time trials. I have no doubt that all these multidirectional movements and sports helped my development in decision-making and anticipation skills, and that utilising the various physical skills aided my progression on the GAA field.

My childhood memories include seeing athletes train and compete at the highest level – from Olympians, such as Paul Hession, Neville Maxwell and Olive Loughnane training in UCG, to GAA inter-county players like Jamesie O'Connor, Seán Óg De Paor and Niall Finnegan. Dad coached lots of GAA teams to success, including Salthill, Castlegar and my own club, Rahoon/Newcastle.

I loved being around sports teams and playing, chatting and practising with GAA players. I loved how focused they were, how hard they worked and the enjoyment they seemed to get from competing.

I can recall as a twelve-year-old going up to Dangan sports fields and training with these inter-county players. Dad would regularly be managing and coaching the Fitzgibbon, Sigerson or Ashbourne

GAA college teams. I remember doing the warm-up and drills with them and feeling that I could, in time, play at that level. I wanted to be a senior inter-county player – and it was a dream I believed I could achieve.

I would go to Dangan at weekends and spend the whole day watching and learning from the top players. I loved the buzz around team environments. I would collect programmes and be able to recite any team in hurling and football from one to fifteen. I could attend or watch five or six games a week. I wanted to get to that level, and this was great first-hand experience for me to see how these players conducted themselves. I was excited and inspired by what I saw, and it set me on a path to play and practise as often as I could to make my dream a reality.

I loved seeing how much I could improve my skills, how well I could play at different ages and potentially how good I could be. I started hurling at nine years of age with Rahoon/Newcastle and played Gaelic football with Salthill. Dad coached football at Salthill GAA club, helping them to numerous underage titles before reaching an All-Ireland senior club final in 1990. He coached many of the camogie teams my sisters, Susan and Lisa, played on from club to college levels. Susan went on to win minor and junior All-Irelands with Galway and provided me with inspiration and belief that I could also cut it at inter-county level.

Starting secondary school in September 1996 at St Mary's College was an exciting time in my life. I had known about its tradition in hurling and football and that it was one of the top GAA schools in the country. I had witnessed the atmosphere at schools' finals they competed in versus St Jarlath's and St Kieran's, and I couldn't wait to be a part of those days.

I went into a year with 120 boys, only knowing one person from my primary school. A great way for me to get to know others and feel accepted was through sport. I quickly began to excel at football and hurling and made many friends through training and games. We had some great sporting teachers who helped my development, such as Seán Óg De Paor, Liam Sammon, Gerry Dempsey and Enda Mulrooney. I loved having double PE on a Monday with Liam (a treble All-Ireland winner and fantastic person), when we tried multiple new sports like badminton, gymnastics and athletics. I was really inspired by the Galway footballers at the time and to have Seán Óg (double All-Ireland winner and All-Star) teach me science and Gaelic football was incredible. The training and the games and the hurling alley at lunchtime brought me on immensely. We started doing gym work before school in the weights room and this helped my physical development. There were such good people and resources in St Mary's, and I felt really at home in the environment they created.

After competing well against some of the strongest schools that year, I felt confident I could make a Galway underage team. I was being coached at underage level in both hurling (with Rahoon/Newcastle) and football (with Salthill) by my father and other helpful and knowledgeable people, like Pat McGrath, Hugh Grehan and John Heffernan. I was enjoying playing both codes and we had relatively successful years, reaching the latter stages of most competitions.

I set myself the first target of making the Galway Under-14 hurling team in 1997. Thankfully, I performed well at the trials and was picked for the squad for the Tony Forristal Tournament, which was held in September, during which I played at wing-back and centre-back. We reached the final in front of a crowd of 5,000. We were the curtain-raiser to an Under-21 All-Ireland semi-final between Cork and Wexford, and it was a nervy yet exciting experience playing in front of such a big crowd at thirteen years of age.

I started Second Year with a new sense of belief in myself. I wanted to kick on over the winter and become even stronger, faster and sharper. I felt I was becoming something of a leader with both club and school teams. At St Mary's, I was made captain of the juvenile hurling and football teams. I loved the discipline of training and practising every day, and the responsibility of leading by example, encouraging lads to train harder and creating a positive atmosphere in the dressing room.

When the schools playing calendar finished around the end of March, I felt very sharp for the club programme just starting in April. This fed into my confidence going to inter-county trials later that summer. In my mind, I was ready to make the step up to the Under-16 Galway hurling team. I had marked most of the players in competitions throughout the year and had nothing to fear.

I'd set myself the next target of making the Under-16 County hurling team at the end of the Under-14 campaign. The trials went well for me, and I made the team approaching my fifteenth birthday. We played in the Nenagh Co-op Tournament, and I was at corner-back when we beat Cork in the final. It felt massive to win my first All-Ireland title with Galway and I was bursting with pride as we visited a few clubs as part of the homecoming.

I went back into school that winter and to my club Rahoon/Newcastle determined to improve further. I started to do more advanced weight training in the garden shed, under my dad's supervision, as well as specific drills I'd learned from specialist coach Jim Kilty to improve my speed, agility and quickness (SAQ). Jim had done SAQ work with the UCG athletes, and I was fortunate to get some time with him to do some individual work.

At the same time, I was honing my hurling skills at every opportunity against the gable of the house and in the ball alley in St Mary's on my lunch breaks. I loved doing this sort of work on my own and seeing the improvement when I went onto the field. Being sharper, fitter and stronger always gave me an edge. I remember from a very young age doing some form of training on Christmas morning and thinking that no one else was doing it. Dad had instilled this work ethic in me, and I'd seen him training a lot of people and pushing them to the next level in the college and around the county. At the time, I was training four or five times a week practically all year round between school, club and county squads.

I made my senior secondary-school team in Third Year. We reached the Connacht final but were beaten by a stronger Gort team on the day. I was eager to go to Galway minor trials that summer, but Dad felt it was best for my development to wait one more year. I was annoyed, as I felt I could make the panel. Instead, I focused on playing well with Galway Under-16s and Minor A with the club that summer and had some good games at wing-forward. I felt playing many different positions and playing a few years above my age helped me learn and mature faster as a player. Nowadays, a lot of players only play their own age grade, and I feel it takes them much longer to make the step up to adult games, as they are not being tested enough in areas such as anticipation, physicality and decision-making at speed, to name a few key areas. In school, I played two years above my age grade a lot, and the same with my club, which helped enormously in gaining the speed and physicality necessary for adult sport.

In Fifth Year in school, I made the Galway minor hurling team. I can remember sitting in the stand at the All-Ireland hurling final the previous year and watching players I had played with – including Gerard Farragher, Damien Hayes and Richie Murray – and thinking I could compete at that level the following year.

When I got asked in for trials, I was nervous and excited – and then overjoyed when I got the nod from the hugely influential and respected manager John Hardiman. During the minor campaign in 2000, we beat Limerick, Offaly and then Cork in the final in Croke Park.

I had played well throughout but, leading up to the final, I strained my hamstring and missed a few weeks' preparation. I got back training the week before the game but, having inevitably lost some of my fitness and sharpness, I was experiencing a lot of doubt and anxiety around my readiness for the final. This doubt manifested in my performance in the final – I felt very low in energy and confidence, and quite restricted physically. I was fearful of making mistakes. I didn't want to let anyone down and my mind was racing and unfocused. I ended up playing poorly and burst out crying at the final whistle with relief that it was all over and that I hadn't cost us the game.

Despite winning my first minor All-Ireland, I felt disappointed. I didn't enjoy the game because I didn't play the way I would have liked. This was my first real experience of my mindset hindering my performance. I did not know it at the time, but this became a great learning experience for me that I often refer to.

Going back to school, I was determined I was going to learn from that experience and come back to Croke Park an improved player. I vowed to train harder that winter and put in more consistent performances for my school and club. I wanted to show I was better than my All-Ireland performance.

My second year as a minor began with a repositioning to wing-back in a match against Derry. I enjoyed the freedom of the half-back line and the greater involvement in the play. We played Tipperary in the semi-final, and I returned to full-back and played well. We qualified to play Cork in the final, and we were going for a hat-trick of minor titles. I was focusing very hard on putting in a good block of training for the final and ensuring I was as sharp as possible. Being able to prepare without any injuries helped my mindset enormously compared to the previous year. I felt I played close to my potential in that final and, even though we lost narrowly, I felt pride in my performance.

When I look back at that phase of my underage career, I feel that – barring one performance in that first final versus Cork in 2000 – my mind was more of a help than a hindrance. When I knew I was prepared and was performing well in training, I generally performed in the bigger games. I had a good sense of belief in myself, that I could master both my opponent and the challenge of performing under pressure when the stakes were high, while the experience of playing in places like Croke Park was invaluable as a young player.

After completing my Leaving Certificate in 2001, I went to NUIG to study commerce. I was now moving closer to that dream of playing at adult inter-county level. I saw Freshers and Fitzgibbon hurling as a great stepping stone. I played full-back for my Freshers team and went on to play midfield with David Tierney with the Fitzgibbon Cup team; with his courage, skill and athleticism David had helped drive Galway to a senior final in 2001. To be training and playing alongside him a year later was confirmation that I was improving as an adult player.

I marked Galway senior star Richie Murray in the Fitzgibbon game versus UL, and felt I held my own despite us getting well beaten on the day. From this, I was called up to the Galway Under-21 team for trials under John Hardiman and managed to perform well at midfield in several games. I was enjoying the step up in the preparation, physicality and speed of the game.

We trained extremely hard, and I was putting in consistent performances for my club in the intermediate championship at midfield. However, halfway through the summer disaster struck when I broke a bone in my hand through a wild pull in a club intermediate game against St Thomas'. I missed around eight weeks of preparation and was back just in time for a challenge match one week out from the Under-21 final against Limerick. To my surprise, I was named to start the challenge game at midfield and did okay. I was even more surprised to be named to start at midfield in the final. I knew deep down I wasn't prepared, and this led to huge levels of doubt and anxiety leading into a game of such magnitude, and I felt low on energy.

Limerick had a phenomenal team and were going for three-in-a-row. From early on, I struggled with the pace, physicality and intensity of their play. Not surprisingly, I was replaced after twenty minutes. I was devastated as I left the field so early in front of nearly 20,000 people. I was down for a few days but then gradually I was able put things in perspective. I had made a lot of progress, and to make the Under-21 team in my first year on the panel was an achievement, especially after battling back from injury.

I had to quickly move on, as, six days later, I was picked to play full-back on the Galway intermediate team, managed by Vincent Mullins, who were through to the All-Ireland final. Although still a bit low on confidence, I managed to prepare well, and we won a tight game in Birr against Tipperary, when I did alright at full-back. It was nice to celebrate an All-Ireland win so soon after the huge defeat to Limerick, and it certainly helped my mood and mindset for the coming weeks.

I finished out the intermediate competition with the club and then decided to knuckle down for the winter and show what I could do with the college and club at Under-21 level. I was training with the Fitzgibbon team for the winter when our manager, Conor Hayes, was appointed Galway senior manager. I knew if I could show my attitude and good form to him, I might be in with a chance of a call-up to the seniors. I played well marking Tipperary star forward Eoin Kelly in a challenge game against Limerick IT in December, and, to my huge delight, I was asked into the senior panel around that time. This was such an exciting period – to be training with legends like Ollie Canning, Kevin Broderick and Eugene Cloonan, from whom I learned so much in terms of leadership, punctuality, communication and preparation.

In 2003, I made my senior league debut against Dublin in Pearse Stadium. I tried to treat it as any normal game, keeping to my routine in college and around training. I had confidence that I was as good as any Dublin player I might be marking, and I was pleased to be playing in the half-back line with plenty of experience around me. Players like David Tierney, Fergal Healy and Ollie Canning were very encouraging to me as a younger player, and I felt part of the squad from early on.

In the game, I played solidly enough at wing-back – I managed to get on a few balls and do the basics well, and I got involved as often as I could in helping the team. We won well, and I was buzzing after it as we went for a few drinks together. We faced a step up in challenge for the next game – Kilkenny in Nowlan Park, the reigning All-Ireland champions. I found the cuteness of John Hoyne too much at times and ended up being substituted in the second half. I wasn't too despondent, as I knew it was a great learning experience.

The next day out, I was sharper and more aggressive and acquitted myself well against Clare in Ennis. I felt at home in the squad and was looking forward to the championship and fighting for my spot on the team. I was placed at number six in training and games and felt I was really coming into form and was picked for the opener against Clare in Cusack Park. We performed well in a red-hot atmosphere and won narrowly. I was named Man of the Match. Life felt good.

In our next knockout game, a preliminary quarter-final in what turned out to be a full crowd in Pearse Stadium, I was marking Conor Gleeson. My confidence was high, and I did well on aerial ball, distribution and reading the game. Halfway through the second half, I was switched over to mark John Carroll, a very direct player. We lost the game by one score. I got very upset that our year was over, but, after a few days wallowing, I decided to reflect on my year.

I felt I had matured as a player and person on and off the field. I had taken on a lot of responsibility as a nineteen-year-old playing in the pivotal number-six role and felt I had acquitted myself quite well. I was proud of how I'd integrated into the squad with many more experienced players and did not let it overawe me, and I was looking forward to building on my form with the Under-21s for the rest of the summer.

We had a great management team led by John Hardiman and were confident we could win an All-Ireland. We beat Tipperary in a great semi-final after extra time and then faced a Kilkenny team that featured many players who would go on to dominate senior hurling for years to come, including Tommy Walsh, J.J. Delaney and Jackie Tyrell. We played below par in the final and Kilkenny won by seven points. It was disappointing, but I had another year at Under-21 and knew I would continue to improve from playing with senior players with club and college.

I found 2004 a bit unsettled. I started the first league game at centre-back and was moved to midfield for a couple of games before losing my place on the team. I was struggling with being moved between full-back, midfield and half-back. I always felt I could make my biggest contributions at number six and found not being able to play there lessened my contribution.

I was in and out of the side that year and was taken off after twenty minutes of the league-final win over Waterford. I was now starting to doubt whether I could perform in national finals, after my negative mindset impacted my performance in the minor final, being taken off in the Under-21 final and now this National League final. I began to have reservations in high-stakes situations.

We had a few weeks' training until the start of the championship. We faced Down in the preliminary quarter-final and, although the team struggled for long periods of the game, I came on at midfield in the second half and did quite well. We managed to win by five or six points to book a place against Kilkenny in the quarter-final. Kilkenny were going for their third All-Ireland in a row, and they blew us away by twenty points in what was a big lesson for the squad in terms of the intensity, hunger and ruthlessness you need to compete at that level. We just hadn't prepared well enough, and a lot of questions were asked of management and players over the winter. Management survived the criticism and the county-board vote and got another term, which was unheard of in Galway at the time. Managers generally got moved on every two years and a whole new plan would be put in place. That lack of continuity or consistency in selection, preparation and personnel had made it very hard to progress as a team.

On reflection, I realise that, at this time, I was putting too much pressure on myself. I was too rigid with my preparation and was not enjoying the journey as I should have. I was telling myself I had to sleep eight hours every night, I had to do three gym sessions a week. I needed to become quicker, to go to the ball alley twice a week. I needed to rest more and stop seeing friends. I started to avoid lectures, thinking that people would just want to talk about the games and this might tire me out. I was doing some sort of training or practice one or two times every day. I was overthinking and overanalysing everything. I didn't play with any freedom or joy that year and struggled for form consequently. I did not allow myself to have any fun in my downtime and felt I couldn't make any mistakes in games, and, if I did, I would work on that mistake constantly the following week to the point of exhaustion.

My mindset was very rigid and one-dimensional. If I got moved position on the field, I would think that management didn't think I was quick enough or experienced enough to play at centre-back. I became fixated on what I was lacking. My internal voice would eat away at my confidence at specific times in the season and impact my performance and enjoyment consistently. I really struggled to manage my internal negative chatter.

Later, that summer, I was made captain of the Galway Under-21 team. It was my final year, and I wanted it to be a successful one. Managed by Vincent Mullins and coached very strongly by Mattie Kenny, we were drawn to play Kilkenny in the All-Ireland semi-final. We were going very well and, ten minutes into the second half, we were six points up playing into the breeze. After that, we conceded ten points in a row and lost by four. This was a very disappointing end to our Under-21 careers, and seeing Kilkenny win the final easily compounded the disappointment. That winter, I graduated with a commerce degree and decided to continue the college life for one more year and do a postgrad in economic science.

In 2005, we started with the same management team for the third year in a row. Conor Hayes had added Seán Silke to his backroom team. Seán would become hugely helpful to me both on and off the field, always offering a word of encouragement when I was down or critical of myself. I was determined to have a much more consistent year. I did a very good block of winter training and was hurling well in Fitzgibbon.

In Dangan, we beat a highly fancied UCC team that included Tommy Walsh, Michael Rice and Tom Kenny, all of whom had played in senior finals the previous few years. We reached the semi-final but were beaten well by a star-studded Limerick Institute of Technology team. At the end of the campaign, I was nominated as a Fitzgibbon All-Star, a huge confidence boost heading back into the Galway seniors following my rocky 2004 season.

I was playing numerous positions for Galway again, but I kept bringing a good attitude and effort to each session and game. We had a patchy league but began to get some momentum in the championship. We beat Limerick by a point in the Gaelic Grounds and that gave us a lot of confidence heading into an All-Ireland quarter-final against Tipperary. I was picked at centre-back before moving to full-back to curtail the dangerous Michael Webster. We came from six points down to win by two points. Those last two games, coming from behind and winning tight contests, built a great spirit in the team.

We now faced Kilkenny in the semi-final. Following our twenty-point drubbing the previous year, many of the local and national media wrote us off. But we played extremely well and won a thriller: 5–18 to 4–18. We had three weeks now to prepare for the big one against Cork, and there was such a buzz in the county. Cork was very strong and experienced, with most of their players holding All-Ireland senior medals from 1999 and 2004. They were going for two-in-a-row and had several household names, including Dónal Óg Cusack, Diarmuid 'The Rock' O'Sullivan and Seán Óg Ó hAilpín in defence, the very fit and fast O'Connor twins and Joe Deane, while Brian Corcoran brought huge class and experience.

In the run-up to the game, there were a lot of external distractions to contend with: ticket allocation, new gear, where we were staying and what we were doing the week after the match. I let these distractions affect me and wasn't as tuned in as I had been for previous games, something that showed in how I started the match. I lacked my usual physicality, and it took me a while to get my hands on the ball, be aggressive with my man and get into the rhythm of my game. I went on to have a solid second half, but we lost the game by four points and felt we had wasted opportunities through bad decision-making and execution.

On reflection, I felt I had a solid championship at midfield, centre-back and full-back. I was nominated for my first All-Star and got to travel on the All-Stars tour to Singapore and meet many players from other counties. We'd lost an All-Ireland final narrowly to Cork, but we were optimistic that we had made big improvements on the previous two seasons. It was a year of many highs and lows, but I was glad to have experienced it.

That winter I graduated from NUIG with a post grad in economic science. I had started as a trainee accountant in DHKN in Galway in September and this was a new transition for me to professional life in the working world. I had a three-and-a-half-year contract with them with the aim of becoming a chartered accountant. I was very optimistic about my life on and off the field.

The winter of 2005 was exciting with a team holiday to China and an All-Star trip to Singapore, and I managed to do a short stint in Thailand with some of my Galway teammates, David Forde, Fergal Healy and Derek Hardiman. The months of December and January were taken up with these trips and we were back into the 2006 season very suddenly with a bang.

In 2006, we were optimistic that we could have a big say in the All-Ireland. But we started the year very poorly, as many of us had been gone for the whole month of January. We were behind the curve with our preparations – again.

We lost our first league game to Antrim and had a patchy campaign. Galway were not in the Leinster championship at this time, and it really hindered our development and consistency as a team. We played a couple of matches against weaker teams before we were pitted against a Kilkenny team that was match-ready in the quarter-final. Their intensity blew us away in the first half. We managed to recover some pride in the second half, but it was too little, too late. They went on to win the final.

Despite our poor displays, I felt my mindset throughout that season was positive and I had played quite well. It felt like a huge step back as a group, though. There was huge uncertainty as management left that winter. Early in the new year, Ger Loughnane the former Clare All-Ireland manager, took over. There was real hope that he would bring the potential out of Galway and end our eighteen-year All-Ireland drought.

We took part in a rigorous training regime for three months, when over ninety players were trained very hard for three sessions a week, with two core and flexibility sessions on two other nights. To Ger's surprise, only one player pulled out of the panel, and he had the task of dropping close to fifty players as we prepared for the league.

It turned out to be a disjointed two years, however, with lots of inconsistent selections, messages and training techniques. We had two very poor championship campaigns and that ended Ger's time with Galway. I had struggled for consistent form in those two years, for various reasons – adjusting to working full-time, doing professional exams and juggling the high demands of travel and training with the inter-county scene. I also had many injuries during this time, having rarely had any before, and they impacted my form and my general well-being day-to-day. I was hopeful that a fresh start would be a good thing for us all.

In the winter of 2008, under new manager John McIntyre, I was not called for the first few sessions. A letter from the county chairman confirmed that I wasn't being considered for the panel for the season ahead. At twenty-four years old, this was a huge disappointment. I felt I had not performed at the level required. I was struggling in my personal life too. I had failed my accountancy exams and my contract had finished after three and a half years. I was finding the move from college difficult. It was challenging to combine full-time work, study and still trying to play at a high level. I had needed to move home, as I was living on social-welfare payments to get by. It was a very uncertain time in my life career-wise, college-wise and sports-wise.

This uncertainty and confusion impacted my mental health. I felt like a failure walking into the social-welfare office and trying to sign up for dole payments. I had been in college for four years and worked in practice for nearly four years, and what had I got to show for it? I had dedicated nearly ten years of my life to being an inter-county hurler with Galway and wanting to win an All-Ireland. I was in a negative mindset and my perspective was focused on what was lacking in my life.

It is during these moments that we all need guidance. Thankfully, I had a caring family and also friends who would give me a little nudge to move on when I was complaining too! I sat with some close friends at the time, Robert Keane and Austin Sammon, who, along with my family, helped refocus me towards my goals.

I had to take responsibility for my actions to pass my exams. Now with no job or inter-county commitments I had more time to dedicate to study.

I had to focus on getting my form and confidence back in order to compete again at senior inter-county level.

I dedicated myself to improving my fitness, speed and strength through the help of Gary Ryan, a former Irish international sprinter, and Fergal Geraghty, a physio from Galway with huge knowledge of the human body. I joined the Galway intermediate team to get competitive matches against senior teams and took on a new role in the forward line with my club. I started to enjoy my hurling again.

I remember a pre-season game in Kilkenny with my club and taking Kilkenny senior James Ryall for six or seven points, which instilled in me the belief that I could get back to that level. I had a decent summer performance-wise for Galway intermediates and the club. I worked hard at passing my exams. By the end of that year, through planning, preparation and execution, I had hit my two main goals: getting back on the panel and passing my exams. It was time to look for a new job as a recently qualified chartered accountant.

In the winter of 2009, I arranged to meet John McIntyre, who was still Galway manager. I decided I needed to be proactive. I had never met him before, and I wanted him to know about my desire to play with Galway. I told John I wanted another chance and that I hadn't yet shown everything I could do in a Galway jersey. If he gave me a chance, I was confident I would make his team better in the season ahead.

A few weeks later, he called me in and told me I was a part of the pre-season plans and it was up to me to make the panel for the league. I trained as smart and as sharp as I ever had that winter, following to the letter the programme that the management team had laid out. I did extra flexibility sessions with teammate Aonghus Callanan. I went to yoga once a week, and loved the mental clarity and flexibility it gave me, under the excellent guidance of Dave Cunningham from The Yoga Shala. I worked harder than ever on my nutrition with team nutritionist Corinna Tobin to get into the best shape possible. I worked on my touch in the alleys three or four times a week. I went to the sea for recovery sessions. I practised visualisation, something I had learned from sport psychologist John McGuire in 2006, and breathwork several times a week. This felt like a fresh start.

I was invigorated by the challenge and the professional setup with John Hardiman and Joe Connolly, great men I respected. I was conscious I needed to prove myself. The team had had a relatively consistent season the year before, losing narrowly to Waterford. I knew there would be strong competition for the backs in the season ahead. I was told I was fourth choice for centre-back but would get game time in the half-back line somewhere in the Walsh Cup, a pre-season competition that started before the National Hurling League.

I got myself fit and sharp for that first game and was picked to play at centre-back when we had a few injuries. It went well and I held my position for the Walsh Cup final where we beat Dublin. I played consistently throughout the league – which we won – and maintained my place for championship, though we lost by a point in the quarter-final to eventual All-Ireland winners Tipperary. That winter, I reflected on the year. As well as Walsh Cup and National League victories, I'd been nominated for an All-Star and was made vice-captain. It had been a huge turnaround in twelve months. I felt I was beginning to show my true abilities in a Galway jersey consistently.

Starting pre-season in winter 2010, there was huge optimism within the squad that we could have a successful year. We felt we could have beaten Tipperary in that quarter-final having led by one point approaching the final minute. To see Tipperary go on to deny Kilkenny the five-in-a-row gave us hope we were not that far away from beating the top teams and winning Liam McCarthy.

We started the league quite well, beating Offaly, Wexford, Kilkenny and Dublin. I was made captain for those games as our captain, Damien Joyce, was out injured. It was a huge honour for me, my family and club, and I felt great trust from the management at being given this responsibility. I played well in those games and was awarded Man of the Match against Dublin and Kilkenny.

We then faced Tipperary at home and were heavily beaten, which was a big disappointment coming close to championship. We had to go to Waterford and win to qualify for a league semi-final, but we lost a close game, and the league finished on a poor note for us.

We had a couple of weeks to prepare for Galway's third year in the Leinster championship. We were pitted against Dublin in our first game. We had a weekend training camp two weeks before it in Johnstown House and trained twice daily. I feel this left us a bit flat heading into the Dublin game and we were beaten by the better team on the day. Looking back at our performance afterwards, we did not have our usual energy levels that we would have expected from ourselves in the championship, and we gave a below-par performance.

Our busy league campaign of travel, training, six league games, going on a training weekend and doing a heavy volume of work had left us very fatigued. The confidence of the squad had already been dented after a poor end to the league, and the defeat to Dublin meant we had to show a lot of resilience to get our season back on track.

We were drawn to play Clare at home in our first knockout game and won well after a stirring performance. Then we beat Cork comprehensively after going four or five points down in the opening quarter. We had now qualified to play Waterford in the All-Ireland quarter-final in Thurles. We had two weeks to prepare for the game and, this time, I felt we took too much time off, feeling we needed to prioritise recovery. We did only three collective sessions in those two weeks and were slightly undercooked. We were underprepared and were beaten by eleven points in sweltering conditions. It was so frustrating to be out at quarter-final stage again. This had now happened in the 2008, 2009, 2010 and 2011 seasons. It was becoming a huge mental challenge, and the pressure was affecting our performances. It felt like we were further than ever from an All-Ireland. Management left after three years in charge – the 2012 season would involve my fourth management team in less than eight years.

I always worried during the winter when the management were leaving. Having been dropped in 2008, I knew the dangers of such changes. Certain players might be blamed for Galway's lack of success and, with the Under-21s winning the All-Ireland in 2011, there would be an appetite for a complete rebuild. When word filtered through that our captain and vice-captain – Shane Kavanagh and Damien Joyce – had been let go, I was extremely annoyed and worried. Others were also dropped, including Gerard Farragher, Eoin Lynch, Adrian Cullinane, Colm Callanan, Donal Barry, Kevin Hayes and Joe Gantley – brilliant teammates who had started the past few seasons.

One day, I got a call at work from an unknown number. It was Anthony Cunningham, the new manager. My heart was in my mouth. He told me I was part of the plans for pre-season, and they would be picking a panel after that for the league. It was up to me to prove my worth. I was relieved, though a little apprehensive about what my role in the squad was going to be.

I once again knuckled down to pre-season. Our first session back was a real eye-opener in terms of the fitness levels the lads wanted us to reach. I was expecting a relatively handy session to ease us back in but ended up getting sick in the first running drill.

Afterwards, we had a team meeting where management outlined their goal of winning Leinster in year one and the All-Ireland in year two. We were then given an outline of the training programme for the next few weeks.

The pre-season went well from a strength and fitness perspective, and we really developed under Kevin Craddock, our strength and conditioning coach. We did okay in the Walsh Cup, trying out lots of players, and I was started at wing-back and centre-back in some of those games. Then Kilkenny beat us comprehensively in the semi-final.

It was now time to focus on the league and, once again, as with previous management, there was a lot of chopping and changing in selection. Lads were given opportunities, but the structure and game plan were a bit disjointed. We had a patchy league and had to win away to Kilkenny to avoid a relegation play-off – instead, we lost by twenty-seven points in one of the worst days for me in a Galway jersey. We had two weeks to prepare for the relegation play-off against Dublin. The management called in more younger players, including Johnny Glynn, Shane Maloney and Pádraig Brehony from the successful minor-winning team of 2011.

My feeling at the time was that we needed more experience, not inexperience. We drew with Dublin and beat them comprehensively in the replay. I felt we were getting a bit more settled in terms of team layout and selection. The positional switches of Kevin Hynes to three, me back to six, Fergal Moore to corner-back, Iarla Tannian and Andy Smith in midfield, Niall Burke at eleven and Joe Canning at fourteen gave us a good spine.

We focused next on championship in Leinster and beat Westmeath and Offaly quite well. We were scoring heavily and getting better defensively as the year progressed. Next up, was Kilkenny in a Leinster final. We had never won a Leinster title, and Kilkenny had already beaten us twice that year, by nine and twenty-seven points respectively, so no one gave us much of a chance. I felt we were in a good position, however. Management had settled on a more consistent team selection, and our training had been sharp and intense. We'd won three championship games in a row and confidence and morale were high. It suited us not to be favourites. We took to the field against Kilkenny believing we could win with the right plan and by bringing huge work rate all over the pitch. We had seen Galway teams do this in 2001 and 2005. It worked and we beat Kilkenny with an excellent performance. It was very emotional after the game meeting and hugging my dad, mum and family under the iconic Hogan Stand. They had supported me through thick and thin. It felt so special being in the middle of Croke Park doing a lap of honour and finally having a victory of real significance together. Having done hours upon hours of preparation and been through many heartaches with the likes of Damien Hayes, Fergal Moore and David Collins, it felt extra special sharing a massive hug with those I had played with from underage up to senior level. It meant so much to have those memories for life together and some major silverware to show for all the dedicated work over several seasons.

We now had five weeks to prepare for an All-Ireland semi-final against Cork in Croke Park. We spent the first weekend playing with our clubs before coming back into camp. We were well prepared and felt we had the quality to win the game – which we did, giving a solid performance and winning by five points.

We were now into our first All-Ireland final since 2005. I was determined that, this time, in terms of mindset and preparation, we would leave no stone unturned.

I emailed management that week to share my experiences of the 2005 final preparations. I wanted to let them know of some of the distractions that could affect us preparing as well as possible for these pressure situations. At this stage of my career, I was very in tune with the mindset required to prepare and perform to a high level consistently. Having worked with two inspiring sport psychologists in Gerry Hussey and John McGuire to mentally prepare for important occasions, and from my own experiences preparing and performing in pressure games, I felt there was a lot I could impart to the group to help us focus on what we needed to do. Part of this was being aware of the many distractions that a final can bring, having been involved in two finals at minor level, two at under-21 and one senior All-Ireland already.

We knuckled down and prepared well. I felt going into the game that the lads were well tuned in. We went up the day of the game and you could sense the buzz, people beeping and cheering us all the way to Dublin. It was nice to get to our hotel and just be in our bubble together before the biggest game of our lives.

I always found these few hours hard enough to pass. After eating, it can take up to three hours before you do your warm-up in the dressing room and on the field. You are trying to stay relaxed but anticipating the game and what might happen. It is difficult to conserve energy as the adrenaline kicks in. We would normally be in the ground for the second half of the minor game. On final day, this could be seventy minutes before we'd go out.

Having a routine planned out of what I wanted to do with the free time worked well for me. I would chat with teammates for a while, stretch and listen to music and try to nap for twenty minutes in the dressing room. As we got closer to warm-up time, fifteen minutes before we went out on the field, I would start to amp things up in terms of getting the body moving and communicating messages with others.

When teams run onto the field on All-Ireland final day, the sound is deafening. The ground is vibrating with the noise of the crowd and, for the first two or three minutes, you can't hear anyone on the pitch. You then start to get into your routine of warming up and talking with the players to tune in to the task at hand.

I feel very fortunate to have experienced this for two minor and three senior All-Irelands. It is a regret not getting to climb the steps of the Hogan to lift Liam MacCarthy, but there is nothing I can change about that now. I felt I gave it my best shot; it just wasn't to be.

We played well in that first final against Kilkenny and were four points up at half-time, but I felt it could have been eight or nine as we controlled large parts of the game. We needed to be more clinical in our finishing and more disciplined in our tackling. In the second half, we tried but didn't seem to have the firepower to put the game to bed, and I felt we didn't have enough experience on the bench to call upon. We secured a draw following a pressure free from Joe Canning. It felt surreal. You build yourself up to win these games and to have no winner or loser leaves things a bit flat.

I felt we didn't get an opportunity to relax that night with our teammates, friends and family. We went to the prearranged post-match banquet and, after it, rather than stay the night and relax, we were on a bus at one in the morning. Most of us didn't get home until three, and I was so tired, I found it hard to sleep.

We had three weeks until the replay, and I remember a lot of the squad being very tired the week after the game. Many came down with flu and other illnesses. The management tailored our training but there did seem to be a lack of energy among us. Then, on the Friday night before the replay our goalie, James Skehill, hurt his shoulder in training. It was obvious he was in pain, and this had an unsettling effect on the squad. He'd been selected to start the replay, but we could all see he was in no fit state, and it was a big shock to see him even togged out. It was a huge error that hurt us on the day. He was taken off at half-time and we were destroyed by a strong Kilkenny team. It was such a disappointing way to end the year and showed how much work we needed to do to beat the All-Ireland-winning teams.

Between 2010 and 2012, I had my most consistent seasons with Galway and was nominated for two All-Stars. We won a National League, a Leinster title and competed in two All-Ireland finals. When I look back at my ten-year career in the seniors, there are a few seasons where I felt my mindset and body were very strong and in sync. I was really focused mentally, I was fit and strong physically, I knew my role and what was expected of me, and my touch was sharp.

I felt in these better seasons that there was greater trust given to me by management. They valued my leadership and input on things, and I felt respected and valued by them. The longer seasons and success helped form stronger bonds together too, and I also felt a closer connection to my teammates.

A major factor in being able to maintain consistency of performance was my mindset, something I worked on from the start to the end of each season. I had only put a proper emphasis on it and lived it when we had a sport psychologist working with the team (John McGuire in 2006 and Gerry Hussey in 2010–2011).

I put huge focus on setting specific and controllable targets for myself on a daily and weekly basis. I worked hard on staying present in training and games through attentional control cues, such as breathwork, trigger words and resetting my body language. I studied my best clips from previous matches to reaffirm my mindset on what I could do. Four or five times a week, I visualised how I wanted to perform. I reflected weekly on my behaviours as a leader, what I did well and where I could improve. I did regular work on the words I was using to describe myself, others and my environment. I focused on the opportunity for growth in each situation rather than dwelling on the negatives. All of this helped me to grow my self-awareness away from a negative mindset to a more empowering one.

My last season with Galway was 2013 and I was very tough mentally. I found it so hard to find any fitness or form that season. I took the 2012 All-Ireland loss badly and, along with my partner being ill at the time, I found myself for several months very low on energy and motivation. Even though I had the tools to help me deal with negative thoughts and my inner critic, I felt burned out, with little energy for work, relationships or sport. The fact we had no sport psychologist in the setup didn't help me recognise the signs in time and utilise the tools I needed to overcome my loss of motivation.

I did not start or play any part in league or championship that season and felt isolated from the group at times. I didn't get anywhere near the fitness or form I'd had the previous three seasons. Every time I pushed myself, in training or away from training, I felt weak and remember stopping halfway through additional running sessions, not being able to continue.

My club form was also poor, and I felt very flat in myself – life felt like a chore a lot of the time. I felt a shadow of my former self. The harder I was working, the weaker I was feeling.

I can remember one weekend where we got knocked out of the club championship on a Friday night. I was asked to do a full session with Galway the following morning at 9 a.m. to catch up. I was spent after it and asked to leave early to meet my life coach, Fran O'Reilly, a very special person who had arrived in my life at a time – in 2013 – when I needed him most. He was a development-of-potential expert, who was working with the Gaelic Players' Association, an organisation formed to help GAA inter-county players develop on and off the field.

On the drive down to meet Fran in Athlone in the Hodson Bay Hotel, I felt very disillusioned with my life. I felt it was unfair to be asked to train the morning after a championship match. This compounded my feelings towards management that they really didn't care about me that season. None of the senior club players would have been asked to train that morning. I felt I was in such a weak position having not played all year and that I had to show I wanted it. It all transpired to drive me further away than ever from the setup.

I was in real need of some support that morning. I was feeling lost and disillusioned in my career, relationships and in life in general. I felt alone and isolated. Meeting Fran that morning and the care and compassion he showed me turned my life around. He began to get me back on my feet again, to help me take back control of my life. It was time to stop trying to please everyone, be it my manager in work, people in my relationships or my hurling management team. It was time for me to do what was right for me, what made me happy and made me come alive.

Fran helped me to see what was possible in my life at that point, that I had some locus of control. It was time to stop being a victim of my environment or other people: it was time to take responsibility for my own success, happiness and wellbeing. I realised I was subcontracting these things out to other people or activities. I was not focusing enough on my inner game, on what made me happy and what made me feel well.

On 23 October 2013, we suffered the tragic loss of our friend and teammate Niall Donohue. Niall was the life and soul of our dressing room.

At the start of November 2013, I was driving home from Dublin, where I had started a certificate course in sports psychology, when my phone rang. It was Anthony Cunningham. He said my form had been poor the past year and that I wouldn't be on the panel for the league and potentially the season. He said he was considering other players and that management would have a look at my club form. I did not believe that he would watch any of my club games. I hadn't seen him at any of my club games in the previous two years he had managed me. I pleaded with him to give me another opportunity, but he wasn't for turning. I knew my time was up with Anthony. It felt like two of the heaviest blows to my heart, losing Niall and losing my inter-county career.

When my inter-county career finished, it left a huge void in my life. Teammates and friends I had seen four or five times a week for close to ten years were now gone from my life. I did not want to bother them while they were in the bubble of training and playing games with Galway. Watching and talking about the team was painful for several years. I was only twenty-nine and felt I had huge value and experience to share within the team. But I knew the door was closed and I needed to move my life in another direction.

Making that call, in April 2013, to the Gaelic Players' Association for information on career development and being put in touch with Fran had been such an important step in getting out of the rut I was in and helping with the transition away from playing inter-county. I am so glad I reached out. Having the support of people like Fran O'Reilly during this time was invaluable.

We sat down for a few hours, and I told him how I was feeling about the loss of my inter-county career. That I was not motivated by accountancy and was wanting to try something new. I told him how I was struggling in my relationships. After a couple of hours, I felt lighter in my mood and outlook. I was enjoying the certificate course that I had been doing at the Institute of Art, Design and Technology in Dublin, and talking things through with Fran, I saw a possibility of doing something new in sport psychology. I began to feel excited and hopeful about my future.

After graduating with a certificate from IADT, I went on to do a master's in applied sport and exercise psychology at Waterford Institute of Technology. This set me on a wonderful path of meeting new people and helping others who might be stuck, lacking clarity and wanting to improve their performance in the important areas of their lives. It has led me to work with some amazing people in sport, business, healthcare and education.

In this book, I wish to share with you what helped me to get my life back from the lows of unemployment, letting go of my inter-county identity and changing my career to make a deeper contribution. I want to show you the key areas to focus on when you are feeling stuck in life, how to get moving and to remain moving in the direction of your goals and aspirations.

Some key turning points in my life

Leaving the Galway inter-county team in 2013 made me reflect on my life and the choices I was making. I had put a lot of energy into being an inter-county hurler from age thirteen to thirty. I realised that a lot of my self-worth had been coming from my performances in sport.

When I played well, I felt good about myself, and felt that I was capable and competent. I also felt good about other people and the world in general. Life seemed a little easier when my sport was going well. When the inter-county experience was taken from me in 2009 and again in 2013, I felt a huge void in my life. I did not really know who I was without the status of being in the team or around it. My life revolved around it and when it was taken from me, I had to reflect more honestly on myself. Who am I? What is my purpose? What do I stand for? What do I believe to be true about myself? What else do I want to experience in my life? What else am I passionate about if sport is not in my life? These were questions I had ignored or had pushed to the back of my mind when I was involved in high-level sport.

The mind is not a static thing. We will move from different mindsets depending on our energy levels, tiredness and what is going on in our lives. This book aims to give you the tools to recognise when you are slipping back into negative mindsets and how to course correct, over time, to get back to where you want to be.

It was easier to tell myself to train harder or to work on my game. I knew how to do that because I'd been doing it since I was a kid. When it came to those deeper questions, I was probably afraid that I did not know the answers. I was uncomfortable with not knowing what might come up and afraid that I might not be able to deal with whatever did come up. What do I really want to do with my life? What else, if anything, am I even good at? Am I able to contribute to conversations, society, relationships and my career when I don't have sport to fall back on?

Meeting with Fran helped me realise that I was only scratching the surface of my potential, that there was a whole world out there for me to explore. I mentioned to him that I loved travelling in the winter months, and he said it was time to get out my rucksack again and start learning about who I am, what I am capable of and how

I might contribute to the world in a different context than sport or accountancy. Starting on this new journey of learning opened my whole world to new experiences, relationships and a career in helping others.

I still regularly feel stuck, uncertain and lost at different times when trying to develop as a person or professionally in an area I do not understand that well. I have come to learn that is the same for most people. I have got better with dealing with this discomfort. The ability to sit with this and question who I am, what I want to do and what I stand for helps me to shed the previous version of me and move to the next version.

I know now that I am not defined by what I do or what happened to me but that I have the power to choose what I want to do now and who I want to be now.

We are never the finished version of ourselves. As long as we can stay open to a growth mindset, then the path will unfold daily for us.

I know that when my career – in both sport and business – was taken away from me on various occasions, it was painful and uncomfortable for a period. It is during these moments of discomfort that we often get to the truth about how resilient we are and what we are capable of. It is a time to reflect on what we have achieved, what we have learned, what we can improve on and what we can let go of to move forward.

When my inter-county career or accountancy job finished, I learned many things about the importance of honest communication, true support from people, committing to something all-in rather than going through the motions, feeling cared for and not isolated, being passionate versus being merely interested – and the effects that all of these can have on life satisfaction, well-being and performance.

After such events in your life, it is important to be compassionate towards yourself. None of us goes through life unscathed. We all suffer at some level, be it career, relationship or sporting pursuits. It is critically important in these moments that we assess our behaviours or performance, not ourselves. We acknowledge the benefits and opportunities that might arise from the experience, and we acknowledge what we can learn from it. Letting go of what we cannot change – what is outside our control – is a vital step in the process too.

I am grateful to the managers, coaches, players and friends who had honest conversations with me and enabled me to work with them in sport psychology. I learned so much from being exposed to these environments on good days, and not so good days. They observed things in me that I had ignored, and therefore had not dealt with. They helped me to find the next path on discovering my potential.

My wish is that this book will help you to unpack even greater layers of the capabilities and greatness that are in you.

How this book works

Imagine what life would be like if you had total clarity about what you wanted to do and how you were going to achieve it. Imagine waking up every morning energised and excited by life and its challenges – with a deep understanding of yourself, your strengths and how they make you unique and special in this world on and off the field.

You know who you are, who you want to be and how you want to live and perform.

You know how to access this deep belief in your own ability and how to strengthen it.

You no longer need outside validation to tell you that you are enough. You give up worrying about other people's expectations of you. You are clear about what success is for you in terms of your life and your sport. You become the person you want to be and live life on your terms, according to what is important to you, and you demonstrate this in every interaction you have.

As you move through your day, you think, feel and move with courage. You speak your truths with no concern for what others think of you. You live life on your terms.

In this book, you are going to achieve clarity on what it takes to be successful. You will develop processes that will enable you to let go of what you can't control and to focus on what you can. By learning how to step into your own values and adapting your behaviour, you will begin to look forward to challenges and events with excitement rather than fear. You will learn how to identify and utilise healthy coping resources to perform under pressure.

My journey began much like yours

I spent almost twenty years of my life trying to manage the challenges of elite sport in Ireland, playing inter-county hurling with Galway. I competed in national finals at every age group, at times in front of crowds of up to 82,000 people. I had moments in my career where negative thoughts and feelings took over, and I choked in front of thousands of people. I could not access any of my skills or my training in those moments, which were very frustrating and difficult to handle.

However, through working with different coaches and sport psychologists, I have learned how to deal with the doubts and anxiety I was experiencing. Coming up to these important occasions, I began to accept my thoughts and feelings in a healthier way, focusing on the opportunity these moments offered rather than perceiving them as a threat or something to fear, and I started to approach them with a new sense of excitement. I began to embrace those challenging situations to see if I could manage and overcome the 'inner worrier' in me.

I became curious to know what strengths I had and where I could grow and evolve to the next level of my potential. Those high-level matches became something to enjoy and learn from rather than something to fear and avoid.

When my time as an inter-county player came to an end after the 2013 season, I went through several difficult adjustments to come to terms with the changes that were happening in my life. It was hard not being a part of the elite team environment, and I missed the preparation, the big games and the friendships. Around this time, I had decided to leave my job as an accountant to pursue a new career in sport psychology. While I was disappointed in no longer being involved as a player, I began to see how I could help people deal with the pressure that comes with high-level sport.

Over the past ten years, I have been fortunate to work with some of the best athletes and teams in Ireland, such as Galway, Tipperary, Limerick and Ballygunner. I have learned so much from them in terms of developing the mental strength to excel under pressure. This book has been a great opportunity to put some of those learnings into a coherent plan that will help you get the best from your life and your sport. By sharing the challenges and experiences I have had on and off the field in a personal, professional and sporting context, I hope they can help you to navigate some of the difficult challenges you might face on your path to achieving your dreams and ambitions on and off the field as a person, athlete or leader in your community.

How to get the most from this book

Every chapter in *MVP* offers two mindsets that compete for your attention. Think of them as two teams playing against each other.

The 'opponent team' is the unhealthy mindset, the current framing that you have on things. This is the mindset that causes you pain and keeps you stuck.

The 'challenger team', on the other hand, is the mindset that you've yet to establish in your life: the healthy framing of situations, the thought patterns and practices that can shift you from feeling stuck and merely surviving to thriving.

By the end of the book, you'll have competed in ten mindset matches:

- Confusion versus Clarity
- Fear versus Courage
- Outcome versus Process
- Threat versus Challenge
- Panic versus Composure
- Doubt versus Confidence
- Pessimism versus Optimism
- Intensity versus Recovery
- Frazzled versus Flow
- Resistance versus Acceptance

To get the most benefit from this book, I encourage you to buy a journal or notebook. As you read each chapter, begin writing things down and encoding them into your mindset, be it the skill of optimism, developing deeper focus or enhancing your confidence. Practise one or two exercises at a time for a few weeks until you have embedded them into your way of doing and being.

For example, in moving to greater clarity in life from Chapter 1, you can use life and sport as an opportunity each day to flex, grow and nourish your values, seeing each situation as an opportunity to develop the person you want to become through value-based intentions rather than focusing on the outcome to be achieved. This will enable you to deepen your character strengths further about who you are and what you want to stand for.

You could look at moving from self-doubt to confidence by listing some previous accomplishments in sport or in your personal and professional life over the past five years, five months or five days. In moving from fear to courage, you can start to recognise your current fear responses when embracing an important situation, acknowledging and validating some of the healthy and unhealthy feelings you have towards certain situations and how they might move you towards, or away from, your values. You can experiment with optimistic expectations – what opportunity comes from being successful in this situation? What could go well here? This will begin the journey of changing how you think, feel and act in moments that are important to you.

Sometimes in daily life, the unhealthy 'opponent' side wins or can dominate your thoughts; sometimes, it's a draw. The aim of this book is to enable you to have a deeper understanding of how your mind works and how to sidestep sabotage when it inevitably shows up – and to give you enough insight to help the healthy 'challenger' side to win often.

My hope is that you will use this book to strengthen those characteristics that serve you well. That you will be able to create clarity in terms of who you are and what matters to you. That you will be clear about what motivates you in your life and will be able to identify the process goals that will help you to achieve success.

I hope you find that you can go back to chapters at different stages to gain greater clarity on your approach and unlock the solutions to your challenges – perhaps to look deeper at your confidence levels, get into the mindset of a challenger or build better concentration.

You might need to renew your inspiration by focusing on what motivates you in life or how to access deeper reservoirs of courage and resilience in the challenging situations you face.

As your levels of awareness upgrade and grow, you can use these chapters to continue to learn, improve and reach new levels of success.

I wish you the very best in pursuing your life's ambitions.

I

CONFUSION VERSUS CLARITY

TO REALLY ACHIEVE MEANINGFUL SUCCESS IN life, it's essential to have clarity about a few things, including who you are, what your identity and your values are, what motivates you and what your goals in life are.

Having clarity about your identity helps you perform better, be happier and achieve more meaningful results. When we don't have clarity around our values, personal goals and our motivation for doing something, we can get sucked into focusing more on what other people think of us – we focus on external praise and validation. In turn, this can lead to performance anxiety, lower confidence, less ambition and consistent negative dialogue with and towards us.

We become distracted by the noise of other people's opinions because we are unclear about our own identity.

In my experience, this outward focus being dominant over inward focus leads to inconsistent performances and, consequently, poorer results.

So, gaining clarity on your identity begins with: 'Who am I?' This might seem like a simple question, but how do most people answer it?

They might start with their name, then their profession, where they live or grew up. They might mention their favourite team or what sport they play. They might mention their relationship status and other roles they have.

None of this gets to the real you.

As humans, we are more complicated than these answers. You are not your name, your job, your college, your place of birth or your gender. Those are part of you, but they don't define you. You are an embodied set of beliefs, values, thoughts, emotions, experiences, wisdom and knowledge. Understanding this is all part of gaining clarity about who you are, where you came from, what you stand for, what you have learned so far in your life and where you want to go.

In this chapter, you will gain a deeper understanding of who you are and what your identity means to you in terms of your values, motivations and goals in life. This will help you to ensure your focus is inward-facing, rather than outward-facing.

Delving into some of your goals in life

If you were to ask yourself what success means for you right now, what would your answer be? Winning that coveted competition or trophy? Buying your dream house? Accumulating wealth, power and respect? To be healthier? To have a better work–life balance? To become a better parent or friend? To have a new car? To gain promotion? To run your own business?

Have you ever asked yourself *why* you want these things? Why do they matter to you now? Are you seeking approval or acceptance from others? Are you seeking external validation? Do you believe you have to win a trophy to gain acceptance, love or positive regard from others? Do you feel you need to achieve certain goals to be seen or heard by others?

If you didn't care about what others thought of you, what would your true vision for your future look like? What would true success look and feel like?

> *What do you care about?*
>
> - *What do you enjoy about life? What brings you joy?*
> - *What qualities do you want to embody in life?*
> - *What do you live for?*
> - *Who do you admire? What is it – either qualities or behaviours – that you admire about them?*
>
> *When you ask yourself these deeper questions again and again, you start to gain greater clarity on why you are here, who you are, what you stand for in life and what you truly desire around your happiness and success.*

When I work with the right formula – focused on clarity (our identity and who we are) rather than confusion (our reputation and what others think of us), I gain insight into what happiness and success are for me, on both an internal and external level. I know why I am here, who I am and what I stand for, and I define a clear process to live in alignment with my vision, purpose, values and goals. This gives my life more meaning, purpose and direction.

My journey to clarity

In November 2008, the Galway panel was beginning training under new manager John McIntyre. I had not been called for the first few sessions and I was concerned. I had been on the panel for the previous five seasons since coming on the senior panel as a nineteen-year-old in 2003. John was the sports editor of the local newspaper, the *Connacht Tribune*, and had been critical of me and the team over the years for our inconsistencies. I was unsure as to how he felt about me as a player.

The following month, I received a letter from the county chairman saying that I wasn't being considered for the Galway senior panel for the season ahead. At twenty-four years of age, this was a huge disappointment and setback. It would be the first time since I was thirteen that I wouldn't be involved in a Galway hurling setup. Although my form had dipped the previous two seasons under Ger Loughnane's management because of injuries, loss of confidence and not being selected to play, I hadn't really considered that I wouldn't be on the panel that year.

I felt shame and embarrassment about how the previous few years had gone, that I had not done myself justice, given the effort I had put in. I was not performing consistently enough to a high standard.

Over the next few months, I struggled a lot in my personal life. In October 2008, I received the results of my final accountancy exams, and I had failed. The contract I had with my employer as an accountant was finishing in March 2009 – I would be unqualified and unemployed.

I had taken three major blows in a couple of months. I felt huge uncertainty and felt a loss of hope for a while. This uncertainty around my professional and sporting career impacted my mental health negatively. I had found the move from college to combining full-time work, study and trying to play GAA at a high level very challenging over the previous three years. These setbacks were all a culmination of underperforming in my exams, my job and my hurling career.

I had some tough decisions to make. I would no longer be able to pay rent and other bills, so I moved home (I was living on social-welfare payments to get by during the economic downturn in the country).

It was a very uncertain time in my life.

I was unsure if I would ever get the chance to play with Galway again. I was uncertain if I really wanted to be an accountant after four years in college and three and a half years, accountancy training. I was feeling completely lost.

My belief system – my belief in who I was – was being tested. I had, up to that point, believed I was a very capable person, but now I felt like a failure walking into the social-welfare office and signing up for dole payments. What had I got to show for four years in college and nearly four working in a practice? I had no professional accounting qualification. I had dedicated nearly ten years of my life to being an inter-county hurler with Galway and wanting to win an All-Ireland and now that looked unlikely.

I was questioning my capability as an athlete and as a person. This was my negative mindset and outlook at the time. My perspective was focused on what I didn't have in my life. I was listening to my self-limiting beliefs about myself, that I was not good enough as a hurler or an accountant. I was telling myself that my managers in sport did not believe in me and that sport was unfair, and that I was not getting rewarded for the hard work put in.

It is in these moments that we all need genuine care, compassion and support. I was fortunate with the family and friends I had around me, who gave me support, but who also gave me a little nudge to move on and pursue new goals when all I was doing was complaining.

During this low period, I found myself reverting to the work I had done with sport psychologist John McGuire during the 2006 season. This became so important in moving me from confusion to clarity.

To get all my fears, worries and concerns out, I began to journal about what I was believing, thinking and feeling about my career, sport and life in general. I began writing out my goals for the short, medium and long term in these three areas. I wrote about why these goals mattered to me. The key actions that were required for me to move forwards. How I was behaving and what was hindering me from moving forwards.

This helped me create a deeper awareness and clarity about what I truly wanted in my life. It helped me to challenge some of my negative thinking patterns and to focus on the skills, qualities and opportunities I did have. It helped reaffirm that I could do the things I wanted to do. It was up to me to bring the right attitude and process. I had a choice: I could remain stuck by blaming others and complaining about my situation or I could choose to take responsibility for my actions.

By leaning on my positive life experiences and previous accomplishments, I could identify the enabling beliefs that I had.

From this more positive perspective, I decided that I could pass my exams if I truly wanted to. I had done so before, and with no job or inter-county commitments I had more time to dedicate to effective study.

I had proven I could compete at senior inter-county level. I was an All-Star nominee and had won All-Irelands at Under-16, minor and intermediate level. I had captained my county at Under-21 level. I was a colleges All-Star. I had won a senior National League and played in an All-Ireland senior final. I had lost my form and confidence for a while, but I believed they could return with the right process in place. The only thing stopping me was me!

I decided to break the big goal of getting back with Galway into smaller short-term goals. I would dedicate myself to improving my fitness, speed and strength through the help of sprint coach and ex-Irish Olympian sprinter Gary Ryan and sports medicine practitioner and friend Fergal Geraghty. I worked on flexibility with Dave Cunningham in the Yoga Shala in Galway. I went to Karen Clancy for energy healing through acupuncture, cupping and nutritional guidance. I had a burning desire to experience again the adrenaline and excitement of playing in Croke Park on All-Ireland final day and giving it everything.

Another key decision was to continue playing at a high level where possible. I joined the Galway intermediate team to get competitive matches against senior teams in the summer of 2009. I took on a new role in the forward line with my club and started to enjoy my hurling again.

Playing in the forwards gave me a sense of freedom that I wasn't marking someone all the time. I could move to different areas of the pitch to be continuously involved in the play. I had a decent summer performance-wise for Galway intermediates and the club and I felt confident that the call might come for the 2010 season.

By June 2009, I had also started to commit more to my studies. I had two exams to repeat in August and not working allowed me the time to focus on them. Having the right attitude, plan and process improved both my motivation and my decision-making.

By the end of that year, through planning, preparation and execution, I had hit my two main goals: I was asked back onto the Galway senior panel and I passed my final accountancy exams.

I was thrilled with these outcomes after a very testing twelve months.

During this period, through journalling, I really drilled down into who I was and what I felt was important – and hurling for my county was a big part of this. I wanted to challenge myself to see how good I could become. I loved being part of a team environment, taking on challenges together and, through high standards, improving one another. I wanted to be part of a team that would inspire the next generation of Galway hurlers to be the best they could be and to challenge for top honours. I wanted to experience the build-up to big matches, and I wanted to make my family, friends and community even more proud of who we are and where we come from.

Having this clarity around what I valued spurred me on even more. Up to that point, I had just floated from setup to setup and from season to season without truly reflecting on why I was doing it or what it meant to me. With this new clarity, I was more focused and driven than ever before.

I had always been driven but whereas before I was trying to avoid failure by trying to prove people wrong, now I was playing for the love of the challenge, the team, expressing my strengths and feeling pride at conquering my own fears and doubts.

What do others think of you?

How might you answer the question: What do others think of you?

You might start with how you want people to see you – as honest, healthy, happy, kind, successful, a good parent, a good partner, a good friend, positive to be around, encouraging to others, helpful, consistent, fair.

You might follow this up with some of the negatives: stubborn, not present, too hard-working, not attentive, not supportive, always on, disconnected, too serious, closed off.

You hope people see the positives but worry that they don't.

Most of us care deeply about what others think of us. We want to feel that we are enough, we want to fit in, to belong. We want to be seen, heard and noticed.

This can be an issue for us all: when we become more concerned with our reputation than our identity, then performance suffers.

Where do we stand on the reputation versus identity spectrum when faced with challenges in life?

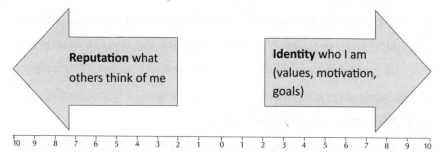

As young kids, we are all about identity. Whether we are playing or throwing a tantrum, we are unconcerned about our actions; we are less affected by what others think of us.

As teenagers, we begin to care. We stop playing with a carefree attitude and turn our concerns to our reputation.

This can be amplified by social media, which prompts us to compare and judge ourselves and others. We are bombarded with messages about what success is, what happiness looks like, how we should look, how we should act, etc. We stop drawing from within our own insights, and so it is no longer about what *we* care about, it is about what *others* care about. This can lead to lower confidence, reduced ambition and a negative inner dialogue about our capabilities.

Caring about reputation is one type of extrinsic motivation, as it comes from external sources, whereas intrinsic motivation comes from within a person. Research suggests that the more intrinsically motivated we are, the more persistent we are in the face of challenges and the more enjoyment we get from our pursuits. Intrinsically motivated people can also experience longer participation and achieve greater progress.

By digging into more of our motivations about why we do certain things, we can learn to lean more on intrinsic factors, and this helps us to focus more on our identity than our reputation.

If we are not clear about these motivations, reputation anxiety can consume high-achieving performers in sport, work and life, even those who you think are immune.

The reason I was dropped from the Galway panel in 2008 wasn't solely down to the previous manager or the new manager – it was down to me. When I was not selected, I went into a downward negative spiral: Why me? How come the management don't believe in me? Am I not good enough? At that time, I did not have the awareness or tools to spot these negative thinking cycles and the damage they were doing to my confidence and sense of hope about the future.

I was too locked into what others thought of me. I did not have clarity about why I wanted to be part of the team. Why did I value it? Why did it matter to me? What does sport, playing for Galway, mean to me? I had lost sight of my own strengths and capabilities. I worried more about what others thought of my performances than I did about my own standards and what I expected from myself and the passion, dedication and commitment I brought to the team.

I believed that others were totally responsible for my success and that when they didn't deliver, life was unfair, that I was being blamed for the team's limitations. I was spending too much time and energy seeking acceptance from others, be it management, coaches or supporters.

While I didn't know it at the time, I was not connected to my true self and was deeply confused about my life in general. I felt disempowered and had begun living in 'victim mode', blaming everyone other than myself for my circumstances. I would later recognise this and take steps to change it. Accessing this clarity about myself, as a hurler and as a person, changed how I approached the game.

I wanted to show the best version of myself and what I was truly capable of. I was aware of people in my own parish who said that I would never make it back, but I wouldn't use this as my motivation.

Recognising negative mindsets

Where do negative mindsets come from and how can we overcome them?

We all have conversations with ourselves each day. It is believed we have somewhere in the region of 60,000–80,000 thoughts per day, some of which are positive, some negative and some neutral. About 90 per cent of these thoughts are said to be repetitive, and almost 70 per cent are considered negative. Our thoughts can form some of our deepest beliefs about ourselves, other people and the world we live in.

Here are some examples:

- **Beliefs about goodness** A person's belief that they are good or bad or that other people are mostly good or bad.
- **Beliefs about likeability** Beliefs such as 'I am unlovable' or 'I am likeable'.
- **Beliefs about the world** Beliefs such as 'The world is a dangerous place' or 'The world is fundamentally unfair'.
- **Beliefs about competence** Beliefs such as 'I am intelligent and resourceful' and 'I will succeed if I try hard'.

These core beliefs come from our experiences, and most are picked up from the environments we grew up in, who we surrounded ourselves with and what we tended to listen to.

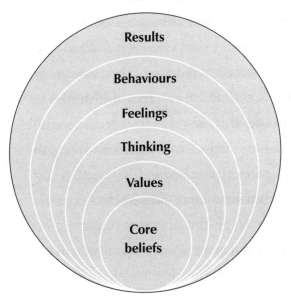

Our core beliefs and values are the foundation of our identity; they drive our decisions and behaviours. They are the guiding principles that give our life meaning and purpose. As you can see from the diagram on the previous page, our core beliefs heavily influence our values (what we deem right or wrong), our thinking, our feelings and our behaviours, which, in turn, influence our results in life.

Your core beliefs are the things you accept to be true, often without question. They are formed throughout your life and are influenced by how you were raised, the positive and negative events in your life, how you have educated yourself on different matters, the results you have achieved in sport, education and your professional career and the use of your imagination around your future success. Your beliefs can affect your moral compass (what you deem right or wrong, good or bad). They are generally assumptions that we have about ourselves, other people and the world, and are not always factually true. Beliefs underlie and influence our values.

Personal values are the things you believe are important in the way you live. They are the behaviours and attributes that guide our decisions and motivate us to act. They serve as guiding principles to our actions and decisions. They differ from person to person, but they are one of the key aspects that makes us all interesting and unique. They are shaped by our culture, religion, education and experiences, particularly during childhood.

Let's use a personal value like honesty.

You feel it is deeply important to always express yourself openly and honestly, to say who you are without fear or compromise. When you do not do this, you feel disappointed in yourself. You might have held back in the past, such as not telling your manager or coach how you feel when you are not included in the team.

Another example is commitment. You want to give 100 per cent commitment in any situation. At work, you are not that passionate about a project you are working on and so you don't give 100 per cent of your effort to it. You then feel disappointment at your lack of effort. You might be picked in a certain position in training, but you don't want to play there. You fail to commit 100 per cent to that position and are disappointed leaving the session.

What are the sources of my core beliefs?

Our core beliefs are usually formed in childhood. They are influenced by the people you surround yourself with or admire from a distance, including authority figures such as a parent, teacher or religious leader, by evidence of something that was proven to us, a revelation that occurred to us from a hunch or divine inspiration, and by the traditions of our family and society.

Our core beliefs have different categories:

- **They can relate to the self and can be positive or negative** 'I am strong' or 'I am weak'; 'I am smart' or 'I am stupid'; 'I am capable' or 'I am incapable'.
- **They can relate to others** 'People like me for who I am' or 'People do not like me'; 'People can be trusted' or 'People cannot be trusted'.
- **They can relate to the world** 'The world is full of adventure' or 'The world is full of danger'; 'The world is full of opportunity' or 'The world is unfair'.

- **They can relate to the future** 'The future is bright' or 'There is no hope for us'.

Beliefs can be enabling or limiting. Enabling beliefs generally display positivity, optimism about the future and confidence in our ability to succeed. They are the positive 'I am' statements I say to myself: 'I am capable, resourceful and intelligent'.

Limiting beliefs can hold us back from realising our potential. We believe they are true even though they are largely inaccurate and unhelpful to us. Individuals with such negative beliefs can be judgemental of themselves and others: 'I am not smart'; 'I am incompetent' or 'I always fail' are common examples.

Our personal values are the core foundation of our identity. The strength of any house is its foundation. The more we become aware of our foundation and work to strengthen it, the stronger and more competent we will feel. We will feel more fulfilled in everyday pursuits and success will feel more meaningful to us. Our relationships with others will feel more significant and our optimism about the future will grow. Our life will have greater purpose and direction. If we don't define our values, we may accidentally violate them and end up feeling guilty, ashamed or embarrassed, but not know why.

When you lack clarity around your core beliefs and values, and what you want for your life, you might feel a range of emotions: frustration, anger, sadness, depression, confusion, a sense of feeling stuck in your life, helplessness or hopelessness. When we experience these unhelpful emotions, we can often adopt negative beliefs about ourselves, others, the world and our futures from them. Adopting beliefs such as 'I am not good enough' or 'My coaches are unfair' or 'I will never get the opportunities that other people get' will have a big impact on the levels of success you experience.

I might value hard work as one of my core values but because of the limiting beliefs I have about myself, others, the world and my future, and the negative thoughts and emotions I am experiencing, I cannot give the required effort and hard work that I want. This then impacts my thoughts and how I am feeling, and my subsequent behaviours and results are impacted greatly.

Nobody likes feeling this way, so the thing we want to be successful at now becomes a source of pain and, to avoid this pain, we might withdraw physically or emotionally to protect ourselves. We find it hard to speak honestly about how we are feeling, and even though we value hard work, we might find ourselves cutting corners, operating with a lack of energy or enthusiasm.

Acting in a way that directly opposes a strong value we have, has a negative impact on our mental health and overall wellbeing.

As an athlete, health is an important value, but if we are operating from a negative belief system, it can be impacted as we lean on substance abuse, such as drink or drugs, gambling or over- or under-eating in order to mask the pain we are experiencing. It goes without saying that the risks to our sporting performances and our mental health are very high if we let things go unresolved.

Mentally you may feel unsure and uncertain about the way forward or how you are even going to start again. You have difficulty concentrating and can feel unfocused, irritable, moody or groggy.

It is difficult – almost impossible – to train and play at the highest level when you are feeling this way. And while I hadn't realised it at the time, I felt all those things in 2008 and 2009, and I had no idea what was causing it. I felt a lack of control over my future, a lack of belief in who I was and a lack of certainty around the direction I wanted to go, and this affected my performance on the pitch. To have clarity and to perform consistently on the pitch, I needed to access my belief system, to be more aware of who I was, what my motives were and what my life goals were.

It is normal to feel confusion, uncertainty and hopelessness at times. It is part of the human condition. In 2008, I was studying to be an accountant, and while I went on to resit my exams and work in that field for the next six years, looking back I was living my life with a vision of who I thought I *should* be – a professional accountant on track for the big house, car and stable career. I was unhappy – deep down, I felt like I wasn't in control of my own future, and that was affecting every other aspect of my life, including my performances on the pitch.

I was uncertain about who I was and what mattered to me, and to feel good enough, I was looking for acceptance from others.

My perspective at the time was that I valued a secure and steady job. This would fit in with my training and I would have a consistent routine. People would view accountancy as a steady career with many options. At the time, it mattered to me what people thought (I was overly worried about appearing capable). I was probably trying to please others by doing this work and it didn't mean the same to me. I was staying quiet and doing all that I was asked to do but never exceeding anyone's expectations with my performances. I let on that I was doing well and did not want to show any weakness. Most days, I was struggling to motivate myself to do the work or study for exams.

As a child, I had learned just to get on with things. If I lost a match, just get on with it. If I was struggling at a subject, just get on with it. If I fought with someone and was angry after, I just learned to bottle everything up and say nothing to anyone. Not happy with my job? Just keep the head down and say nothing. Struggling with a lack of feedback? Just keep the head down and say nothing. I wanted to say things, but I always found a reason why I shouldn't be vulnerable.

It took me a long time to move away from these conditions that I had put myself under. I was using my career to feel worthy or enough. I was using sport to feel worthy or enough. When I had a good day or performance, I felt good about myself. When things went bad, I felt disappointed, and sometimes broken. It took a lot of work to acknowledge this and to begin to heal from this negative blueprint. I had to move my belief system to a new enabling belief system: one in which I believed that I was a lovable and capable person regardless of my job or how I performed in a match.

Today, it can be harder than ever not to adopt society's beliefs and values of success. We get bombarded with so many messages about what success means, from a career, relationship, physical appearance and lifestyle perspective. We are living in an age of social-media influencers and it can be difficult to understand what we want from life versus what society deems we *should* want. It can be difficult to distinguish between what will make us happy and the short-term fixes of social validation from external influences. With all the quick fixes and hacks for happiness, health and success, it can be harder than ever to have clarity around what we want to stand for, achieve and experience.

When change is happening it can be hard to know what 'better' looks, feels and sounds like. We search for answers outside of ourselves but often our innermost values and beliefs don't align with what society is telling us. To get clarity around what matters to us, and to bring this clarity onto the playing field, we must explore our values.

Mental training

To move from confusion to clarity, we must identify our core beliefs and values.

A personal value is a deep belief that shapes your behaviour. Personal values should determine your priorities and how you choose to live your life. When the actions you take and the things you do are in alignment, there is a happiness, harmony and flow to life. When you behave in ways that are not true to you and do things that you do not value, you experience unhappiness, disharmony and unease.

Values can be broken down into two areas.

Firstly, moral standards of behaviour – for example being kind to people, having integrity and respecting other people's ideas, background and culture. Secondly, the elements of life that we value most – for example our health, being a loving parent, our family and our career. Values provide us with direction about how we want to behave and what is important to us in our life – what we value and what is meaningful to us.

It is easy to get caught up in the demands of life, be it career, finances or sport. We can often lose perspective about the things that bring true inner happiness and that make life worthwhile. It's vital that we take time to determine what is truly important to us and to begin living our lives according to the values we hold dear.

In this section, we will focus on those areas in life that we deem important right now. For some, being a good parent is a high priority. For others, being healthy is a high priority and those people will often run or lift weights to feel good. Our values can require effort, may not be easy and can be hard to define at times.

Sometimes, we confuse goals with values. Our goals should feed our values. If being healthy is a value, then goals like playing sport or running a marathon feed that value. Values are the why, goals are the what.

Below we will look at establishing your values and how you can incorporate goals into your daily life to achieve those values, thereby creating and living your life with clarity and not confusion.

It can be difficult, given the fast-paced nature of modern life, to take time to critically reflect on your life experiences. But it can be extremely beneficial to do so, and a great way to highlight your inner strength and resilience in tough situations. It can also uncover some of your most important moral values.

Looking at your life as a river is a great analogy: you can see where you have been flowing or where you are stuck or where you overcame obstacles or where you gently meandered along. It can highlight where you took different routes to success and the lessons that unfolded from those routes. Success is never in a straight line!

The following exercise, which is adapted from Joyce Mercer, is a great way to identify some of the strengths we have, the support we have got from others, the difficulties we've experienced and, consequently, what our beliefs about ourselves, others and the world are. It will give you a clearer perspective on your beliefs, your values and the direction in which you want your life to go. It can help you make greater sense of and speak about your past more freely and compassionately.

Exercises

EXERCISE 1: LIFE AS A RIVER
- Identify the times in your life when you felt most happy, proud and fulfilled?
- Break down your life into five- or ten-year blocks – for example childhood, teenage years, college, career, etc.
- Identify what you were doing. Who was there? What impact, both positive and negative, did events have on you? What did you learn from each of the main events? What did you value after that experience?

EXERCISE 2: LIST YOUR VALUES
To help us to get more clarity around our priorities in life and to not get dragged along by social media and other people's opinions,

please use the following exercise to focus on the things that you deem are the most important to you. Circle a number for each value to show its level of importance to you. Feel free to add some of your own values to this list.

VALUE	LOW TO HIGH IMPORTANCE
Health	1 2 3 4 5 6 7 8 9 10
Family	1 2 3 4 5 6 7 8 9 10
Friends	1 2 3 4 5 6 7 8 9 10
Career	1 2 3 4 5 6 7 8 9 10
Community	1 2 3 4 5 6 7 8 9 10
Education	1 2 3 4 5 6 7 8 9 10
Spirituality	1 2 3 4 5 6 7 8 9 10
Adventure	1 2 3 4 5 6 7 8 9 10
Romantic partner	1 2 3 4 5 6 7 8 9 10
Nature	1 2 3 4 5 6 7 8 9 10
Contribution	1 2 3 4 5 6 7 8 9 10
Other	1 2 3 4 5 6 7 8 9 10

From the list, pick your top four values. Write these down and then write down what you need to be doing for each one right now if you were living these truthfully. Write down some activities or behaviours you would do on a regular basis that would reflect your values in different areas.

Now, take some time to think about what it would be like to be living each value authentically. How would it make you feel if you were doing these things consistently?

Looking back over the past week, how have you performed, out of ten, in relation to these values and the actions that feed them? What has gone well and what can be improved for next week? How can it be improved on? See the example below.

VALUE (TOP 4)	HOW DID I PERFORM THIS WEEK?									
Health	1	2	3	4	5	6	7	8	9	10
Family	1	2	3	4	5	6	7	8	9	10
Career	1	2	3	4	5	6	7	8	9	10
Community	1	2	3	4	5	6	7	8	9	10

This is not about perfection. At different stages of our week, month or life, certain values may take on added significance and we may not have the time or capacity to feed other values. This is perfectly normal. Do not be critical of or harsh with yourself. There will always be opportunities to try again.

When working with sports people, I tend to focus on one or two areas very methodically at certain stages of the season to ensure adequate time and effort is given to their goals and development in that area. That is the nature of wanting to succeed at something worthwhile to you.

It is important, however, that you also find ways to feed and nourish other areas of your life that are meaningful to you, even in a small way. This can renew energy, motivation and a determination to devote time to other important pursuits on your journey to success.

When we align our energy, attention and behaviours to what

matters to us, we begin to see the world in a new light. Each day is an opportunity to decide how we want to live. We have the choice to devote our time and resources, for example, growing our health, relationships, career and having a stronger impact in society.

When we have this clear vision of what matters to us, we experience greater meaning and purpose. We are not living on autopilot; we are intentional and deliberate about how we spend our time and resources.

EXERCISE 3: LIVING OUR VALUES

How can we grow and feed our values? Spending time with friends or family, exercising more consistently, being a loving partner, having a cleaner home and helping in the community are examples of how we live our values more deeply. How do we integrate these into everyday actions and behaviours? Go through each of the steps below (you can use the examples on pages 26–28 as a guide).

1. Write down your top three priority values.
2. Write down five small behaviours that support and grow these values.
3. Schedule at least one behaviour per day in each value that feeds and grows that value.
4. Notice how you feel when you engage in these behaviours, and afterwards.
5. Aim to practise one value-based behaviour in each of your top three values daily for a week. Observe how they make you feel, during and after the activity.
6. Practise new behaviours from your list each week.

EXAMPLE 1: VALUES, VISIONS AND ACTIONS

What is success in life for you this year? In order to prioritise your values – the things you believe are important – you need to set tangible goals or visions. These are what you strive for in a given time period, be it a week, month, season, year, etc. The actions are the steps used to achieve your visions. The table below includes four examples of values and visions you might have and outlines the actions that can be taken in order to succeed in your visions. You can write down your own values, visions and actions if you wish.

VALUE	HEALTH	FAMILY
VISION	To be the healthiest I have ever been	To be the most supportive husband and father I can
ACTIONS	1. Sleep 8 hours a night, with the same sleep/wake times (to within 30–60 minutes), e.g. going to bed between 10pm and 11pm and waking between 6am and 7am. 2. Meditate for 20 minutes daily. 3. Spend 15 minutes in morning sunlight. 4. Exercise for a minimum 30 minutes daily. 5. Consume healthy and natural foods as often as possible.	1. Spend time being present with them. 2. Do one fun thing together each day. 3. Have one meal a day together. 4. Do a good deed for them. 5. Check in and see how their day went. 6. Tell them I love them daily.

VALUE	COMMUNITY	CAREER
VISION	To be an inspiring leader to my community	To have a massive impact on my clients' success
ACTIONS	1. Help improve my club's players. 2. Help my club achieve intermediate success. 3. Help my club impact the wider community. 4. Help my club create a positive, safe and inclusive learning environment. 5. Help my club live its core values.	1. Create a book that teaches people how to develop a mindset to transform their life. 2. Impact more people in business through my work as an emotional-intelligence leadership coach. 3. Impact more teams through improving team identity, relationships and performances.

EXAMPLE 2: VALUES, VISIONS AND ACTIONS FOR SPORT

Our time goes fast each day. We tend to spend about eight hours sleeping, eight hours working or in college, one to two hours eating and maybe one to two hours travelling. When we also factor in responsibilities like housework or life admin, the actual free time to do what we want can be as little as three hours a day, meaning our visions for sport can often be neglected.

If we are not careful, we can get dragged along by other people's agendas. When this happens to us on a consistent basis, we can feel exhausted and depleted and no closer to who we really want to become or what we want to achieve. If we are not deliberate and intentional about creating our vision of success in sport, identifying the beliefs and values that will help us on the journey, then we can end up like the leaves of the trees scattered everywhere and making little impact in the world. I believe everyone has a deeper purpose and reason for being here, to have made an impact, be it to be seen, heard, valued, respected or connected, both on and off the field.

Below are some sample values, visions and actions specifically geared towards sport that may help with crafting your own.

VALUE	FAMILY	TEAMMATES	SUPPORTERS
VISION	To make my family proud	To be a positive encourager for my teammates	To be an inspiring role model for supporters
ACTIONS	1. Giving honest effort in everything on and off the pitch. 2. Showing respect to officials, coaches and players. 3. Sharing the successes/ losses with them.	1. Giving positive encouragement even in hard moments. 2. Challenging poor standards that harm them and the team. 3. Checking in to see how they are doing away from sport.	1. Leaving everything out on the field in pursuit of success. 2. Speaking positively about our team and community. 3. Helping out in the club with young players and members.

EXERCISE 4: TESTIMONIAL DINNER

This exercise will help you to think more clearly about the type of sports person or person in general you want to be and the legacy you wish to create. It can be done in relation to any aspect of your life, be it retirement from your professional career, leaving your community or passing on.

Imagine it's the end of your career or it's your funeral. Several of your coaches, club and county officials, family, teammates, opponents and colleagues have been asked to speak on your impact and contribution to your club, community, county and country.

1. What kind of person would you like to be seen as by teammates you trained and played with, colleagues you worked with, by coaches or managers who trained you, by opponents that played against you, by sporting leaders who were a part of your club or organisation, by younger players you encountered, by supporters in your community?
2. What type of person would you like to be for your family?
3. Look for common values and behaviours that show up.
4. Identify the three most important moral values and behaviours that nourish and grow these.

Self-Talk

It can be hard to control our thoughts, but I believe we can have control over what we say to ourselves. We have a choice about what we believe about ourselves, others, the world and our future.

To create a strong and empowering belief system we must regularly check what we are saying to ourselves. Is my inner dialogue leaning towards things I can't do, haven't done and won't be able for? Or is it telling me what I can do, have done and am capable of?

We can work on this inner dialogue through our self-talk. Self-talk is what we say to ourselves on purpose. Thoughts are generated automatically and are not always under our control. Self-talk is something we do; we can become deliberate and intentional about what we say to ourselves. We can use affirmations or positive statements to create new mindsets. We can use statements like 'I am strong, capable and confident' or 'People are generally very kind and supportive'. These statements, over time, and with the right energy, can lead to new beliefs about ourselves and others.

We can use statements like 'The world is full of many new opportunities to succeed and have happy experiences', which can change our beliefs about the world and our future. We can also look for evidence of our capabilities (using past achievements), where people were kind and supportive, and where new opportunities and experiences presented themselves. These reference points from the past are important if we are to change negative mindsets.

On the pitch

An inter-county footballer I worked with was feeling uncertain and confused around a career decision he had to make. He was in an organisation where he felt that, to get promoted or move up the ladder, he had to be deceiving and show others up when he could. It was all about competing and getting one over on the competition. One of his core values was honesty, so this work environment was troubling for him.

My client knew he wanted to step away from the situation. I could see he was deliberating. He was expecting a child with his partner in the coming months, he was undertaking further education and, if he moved now, it would mean more travel to and from work, which would affect the time he had for college on certain days. Would he be able to financially support his family? Would he have enough time to train? Would the extra travel impact his time with his new baby? Would he still be able to play football at the highest level? These were some of the thoughts swirling around in his head daily.

These were all legitimate concerns. We decided to look at how and why he might make this transition away from his job. We looked at what he wanted his life to stand for, regardless of his current roles. What would make him happiest? What would success be for him? His moral values were about honesty and selflessness. In his current role, he felt the environment encouraged dishonesty, where he had to promote his best interests over everyone else's. He no longer wanted to be in an environment that did not align with his values. He committed to stepping away on an agreed date.

The values that were important to him were his health, family, career and sport. We identified the key visions and goals for his life in these areas, and the key values-based behaviours that would enable him to grow and nourish these areas daily.

He was now feeling extremely clear about the person he wanted to be, what he wanted for his life and how he would show, grow and move towards this vision daily. And with that awareness, he stepped into a new role that truly fulfilled him, while also nourishing all his value-driven needs. This had a very positive impact on his happiness, his energy and his confidence, and his performances on and off the field have excelled.

Summary

Am I inspired by my vision of the future or am I being held back by my memories, beliefs and emotions of the past? It is time to create your new vision for your new life and become the person you want to be, someone who feels motivated, energised and excited by the new opportunities and possibilities that are entering your life now and in the future.

To create this vision, you must check if you are in 'victim mode' or 'responsibility mode'. When you are in victim mode, you are attaching your success, happiness and results to factors entirely outside of yourself. When you are in 'responsibility mode', you realise that you must accept the things that are outside your control and then move towards what you can control, right now, in the present moment.

- **Power of choice** We can all choose what we focus our attention on and what we put our energy into each moment we are awake and conscious. Are they things that will move me towards or away from my vision?

- **Values compass** To gain clarity we must have a vision and destination (our goals) and direction (our values and behaviours).

Values are our moral compass that drives our behaviours and decisions. When we know what we stand for and what matters to us, we can start to behave the way we want and do the things that matter. We start to feel in flow and content in life. When we are not behaving the way we want, and not doing what is meaningful to us, then we start to feel unhappiness and unease in life.

When we are clear about our values and goals, we start living more on our terms and in greater alignment and harmony with the natural flow and energy of life. Great things that are expected, and unexpected, begin to happen.

2

FEAR VERSUS COURAGE

HAVING THE COURAGE TO STAND UP FOR WHAT you believe in is one of the most challenging things you can do, but also one of the most rewarding.

When we are faced with challenges in life, we can choose to overcome them or avoid them. We employ either approach behaviours, where we walk towards success, or avoidance behaviours, where we try to avoid failure.

It is very natural for our fight-or-flight response to kick in. There are two parts of our brain that we must be aware of: the prefrontal cortex and the limbic system.

The prefrontal cortex is the thinking part of our brain. It is very good at higher level thinking, such as empathy, insight, emotional regulation and responding flexibly. It can be rational, logical and intuitive. The limbic system, on the other hand, is very good at sensing threat, firing our stress response, bringing drive and motivation.

Fear begins in the amygdala part of the brain that houses emotions. It is often referred to as the threat detector. Located at the back of the brain and linked to our central nervous system, it scans our environment for any threats. It was very useful for our hunter-gatherer ancestors, as it helped them to sense physical threats in their environment as they faced possible death daily. The amygdala is activated when it perceives danger, and it elicits the fear response. This can happen when we are in actual danger and if we believe we are in danger, if we experience scary stimuli, like seeing snakes, or even by our thoughts or perceptions. When we experience fear, our mental processing can slow down, and we can find it difficult to speak or make rational decisions.

In today's world, we face few physical threats. However, the same fear or stress response is activated when we experience emotional threats, for example the fear of looking stupid, the fear of making mistakes, the fear of letting teammates, parents or supporters down, the fear of not living up to expectations and the fear of exclusion. While this fear response is trying to protect us, it can also prevent us from trying new things, from getting outside of our comfort zone.

In trying to protect us, the fear response can keep us stuck where we are, too fearful to take a risk or make a change in our life.

This safe place and comfort zone is not safe at all. It is inhibiting you from real growth, understanding and learning. It is hiding you from your true capabilities, from your true strengths. It will try to stop you doing things that challenge you and make you grow – mentally, emotionally and physically. If we let fear rule our lives, we will never get to experience the satisfaction of triumphing over new challenges or unearthing our full potential.

In this chapter, you will learn how to recognise your natural tendency to be fearful. You will start to accept it, welcome it, feel it – and face your fear response. You will understand how to face rather than avoid fearful situations. You will learn to harness the fear response's energy to facilitate improvements in focus and a determination to succeed, ultimately to become a consistent high performer.

My journey to courage

After making it back onto the Galway squad in the winter of 2009, I felt the previous few years of hurt, disappointment and uncertainty were firmly in the past. There was an entirely new management team with changes to the playing group too. I had some fears about what my role might be and where I was in the pecking order, and I was also unsure how management perceived me. I took a courageous step and spoke with the manager about where I stood. He was honest with me; when I asked about my favoured centre-back position, he said he would try me there or in the half-back line in the early pre-season games. He said I was fourth-choice centre-back but that that could change, depending on performances. I now had clarity on what I needed to do to get on the team. I was excited and ready for the challenge.

The fear and lack of confidence that I had experienced in the Galway shirt from the 2007 and 2008 seasons was still present to an extent, and I knew I had to stand up to my own self-doubt and put myself into the arena of competition.

I worked very hard that winter on my physical and mental fitness. I took time each week to plan how I was going to develop both my game and me into the strongest, most confident and most composed version of myself. I wanted to see if the work I was doing on and off the pitch was working, and I needed and wanted to get a few games under my belt. Would the old fears and doubts surface: 'Am I good enough? Am I fast enough to cope at this level? Will I be able to mark the top players in fast and intense games?' Thankfully, I got a surprise start in our opening Walsh Cup game versus Laois in January 2010. A few illnesses, injuries and college commitments meant I got a run in my favourite centre-back position. I knew this was a chance to show what I could do. I had waited five years for this opportunity, and I was determined to grab it.

I was slightly nervous before the game, which I knew I would be. I had planned for this feeling coming up and felt it in my visualisation practice that John McGuire had built with me in 2006. I concentrated on my pre-game routines. I took some deep breaths to settle my fear response and to stay connected to the present moment. I reminded myself of the character I had shown to get here and that I had played many good games against Laois and could do so again. I focused on my role and the key tasks that would help me perform, such as consistent communication, good body language, positive self-talk regardless of how the game was going, focusing on one play at a time and being relentless until the game ended.

I got on an early ball and settled into the game quickly. I began to read the play well, take down high ball and demand good organisation and concentration from my teammates. I was enjoying the battle in a hard-fought game. I felt fully immersed in each play and had loads of involvements, even managing a long-distance point to cap a solid performance. The game finished a draw at normal time, and I was delighted we got another twenty-plus minutes of extra time to show what I could do. We won, and the feedback from players and management afterwards was extremely positive. I felt I had taken a significant step forward. My mind felt freer on the pitch than it had for a few seasons. I was not hesitant in my play. I was attacking the ball, aggressive in the physical contests, and I was not afraid to demand effort from my teammates. I knew there would be bigger tests ahead for my fear response, but this was a good beginning.

As the season progressed, I felt I embraced the challenges like never before. I had great faith in the preparation I had put in. In 2010, we won the Walsh Cup and National League and reached the Leinster final. I felt the consistency of my mental approach went to new levels. I felt such clarity, confidence and composure on the field. I was winning the battle with myself on most occasions. Unfortunately, we lost to Tipperary in the All-Ireland quarter-final by a point. I was hugely disappointed, as I'd felt we were genuine contenders. I took solace in the fact that I had faced my demons – my fears of not being able to perform, worrying about others, of not being good enough. I had laid myself bare and gone out into the arena and I had conquered myself through acknowledging and accepting my fears and concerns, realising that I had courage in abundance when faced with challenges. We faced more challenges in 2011 with a rocky league campaign and losing our first championship game to Dublin. Our backs were to the wall in our next two knockout championship matches, beating Clare and Cork convincingly. Apart from our last performance in the quarter-final defeat to Waterford, I felt my mentality was in a consistent and strong place for the most part that season. The 2012 season was one in which I aimed for consistency, and after a very slow start for the team in the league we started to put consistent performances together against Dublin, Westmeath, Offaly, Kilkenny, Cork and the All-Ireland final draw with Kilkenny. I felt my mindset was very clear and calm in preparing and performing under pressure through the mindset practices I had adopted diligently in terms of self-talk, refocusing triggers, visualisation, imagery and meditation.

In 2013, my life changed in a major way. I was five years post-qualified as an accountant working in Fintrax (now Planet) in Galway city, working as the finance manager for some of our Irish and European companies. I liked the company and the people I worked for but, deep down, I felt I just didn't fit as an accountant. I rarely read any articles that came through from Chartered Accountants Ireland. I never bought the *Sunday Business Post*. I didn't listen to any podcasts on accounting. Sport was my passion and my release from the sometimes-mundane day-to-day tasks of my work.

I knew that I needed to take a courageous step. I was in a safe place, a comfort zone, and it was hindering my growth as a person because I was stagnating on the inside. I began to look more deeply at what I wanted to do for myself. I asked myself what would make me happy right now? What do I want to put my time and energy into for the next ten years?

Deep down I had known for a few months that I wanted to move from my career as an accountant. I took the first step by meeting life coach Fran O'Reilly through the Gaelic Players' Association player-development programme in June 2013. We identified my strengths and what I was passionate about. An area that had always interested me was the inner workings of the human mind. I noticed several times that when I was positive, focused and strong, good things tended to happen. When I was negative, unfocused and weak mentally, negative things tended to happen. While playing for Galway, I had read sport psychology books, such as *The Inner Game of Golf* by Timothy Gallwey. The different perspectives this book gave me on training the mind were invaluable. I also had good experiences working with two sport psychologists during my time with Galway: John McGuire in 2006 and Gerry Hussey in 2010–2011. They really helped me with my confidence as a person, not just as a performer. I found meditation, visualisation, goal-setting and self-talk very helpful for creating a more focused, calmer and confident version of me.

From working with Fran, I realised that fear was holding me back in familiar patterns and behaviours. I needed to show courage now and take control and responsibility for my happiness and success. I had worked in a safe and secure job the past five years; it was my comfort zone that I needed to break free from. I had not investigated who I was deeply enough. What I valued and cared about. What motivated me and what goals I wanted to achieve. I had stayed in the job because I didn't know what else I could do. I had never really explored what other strengths I had or looked at other areas I was passionate about. That was when I realised sport psychology might be a career that interested me.

In September 2013, I started a course for a certificate in sport psychology at the Institute of Art, Design and Technology (IADT) in Dún Laoghaire. This was part-time in the evenings, every Wednesday for two hours for twenty weeks. Driving to Dublin every Wednesday became my next focus. I began to really enjoy the conversations, learning and activities in the class. I soaked up extra reading and videos around confidence, performance anxiety and team dynamics. I could see a whole new path opening for me. As an accountant, I had studied just to pass exams; the material was uninspiring and simply a means to an end. Learning about the human mind, personality types and mental-skills training, on the other hand, was of huge interest to me. I found myself completely engaged and excited to learn new skills that could benefit me and others.

Then, in November 2013, I received a call from the Galway manager Anthony Cunningham to tell me I was not part of the panel for the 2014 pre-season. My heart sank; it was the second time in my senior career that I had been let go from the panel. I was twenty-nine and it felt like I might not have the opportunity again to put on a Galway jersey and play in Croke Park. I felt sad, despondent and disappointed.

The part that had given me the most fulfilment – playing inter-county hurling – was now gone. I could go on pretending that I was fine, but it was time to be honest with myself. I was drifting along on autopilot. I was in a comfort zone with my career. I was safe and secure but not getting any closer to realising my potential. I needed to do something that was uncertain and that would challenge me. Not being an inter-county hurler meant what? Who was Tony Óg if he wasn't the hurler? What would I be known for now? It was time to move away from what others thought of me and focus on my internal motivations, such as love of learning, embracing new experiences and exploring other parts of my personality and what I found interesting.

In a way, having my career as an inter-county hurler cut short forced me to act. What was the point in staying in a career I was not enjoying? I was enjoying doing the sports psychology course; it gave me a focus. So why not pursue it more? The only thing stopping me was my own fear – what would people think of me starting a new career? What were the past ten years in accountancy all about? Would I be any good as a sport psychologist? How would I make a living? The questions loomed over me, but my work with Fran had taught me to think less on my fears and focus instead on what motivated me and on my goals.

Being dropped from the inter-county team at the end of the 2013 season only helped to solidify my desire to continue my studies and pursue a new career. After I had earned my higher certificate in sport psychology, I enquired about master's programmes in Waterford Institute of Technology (WIT) and the University of Limerick (UL). After speaking with Dr Ciara Losty in WIT, I felt that the course content, experience of the lecturers and application of the performance psychology skills would be something very beneficial and enjoyable for me.

The next step was a meeting with my accountancy manager in work in Fintrax in Galway. I told him about the master's, that it would help me in terms of understanding personality, team dynamics and focus for work. That I would need to take Mondays off during the college year, a week off each semester for residential weeks and time off around exams for the next fifteen months. Thankfully, he allowed this to happen, provided I worked up the time I was away.

I felt so excited leaving the office that day. I was on the next step of my journey to becoming a sport and performance psychology coach. I felt empowered now that I was back in control of my happiness and success. I was back making the decisions that were best for me at this stage of my life. This came, I believe, from moving away from the security of what I had always known and instead trying something new. I had found something I had an interest in and through which I could see a pathway towards helping others. Building my competencies in this new area gave me a lot of confidence. I was hugely excited to be embarking on a new and potentially rewarding journey.

Recognising negative mindsets (recognising fear)

What can happen to us in sport if we are in a comfort zone? The comfort zone is a mental state where we feel safe and at ease, which is a basic human need. When we are in our comfort zone, we know what to expect and how to react. We are in control. However, when we leave our comfort zone, we do not feel we are in control in any situation. Our brains have not yet created the pathway for how it needs to react, and we may experience anxiety, confusion and fear.

We all have a need for expansion of our current capacity, understanding and capabilities. When we move out of the familiar comfort zone, we are experiencing the tension between certainty and uncertainty, we are moving from comfort to discomfort.

For a sports person comfort zones are extremely important in terms of rest and recovery, such as sleep, time with family and

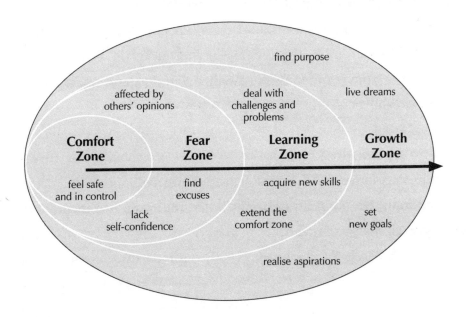

hobbies. It is also extremely important to become comfortable with uncertainty, the unknown and discomfort, and to find new ways to explore discomfort through challenging tasks in the gym, on the field or discussing issues with management. To feel some fear and discomfort, we must expose ourselves to failure on a consistent basis and become self-aware about how we handle it, cope with it and learn from it.

Through these discomforts and failures, you can move to the next level of your potential. What are the areas of your training and performance that you feel less certain about? What emotions do you experience when you think about or do these things? What is your dominant response towards failure: are you aggressive towards it, passive towards it or do you try to escape from it? How do you currently deal with challenges outside your comfort zone: avoid the task or walk towards it? What are the healthy and unhealthy coping responses you currently use? What way might you like to respond to failures or discomfort in the future – for example, this is complex and uncertain, but I know I can grow from it and move further in my understanding, capacity and capabilities?

Mental training

What is courage? Well, for me, it's the ability to do something that's important for yourself, especially when the route is difficult and success is not guaranteed.

Psychologist S.J. Rachman (1990) outlined three components of fear:

1. The 'subjective feeling of apprehension', which may cause worry and unease about an upcoming event, for example a match, and what failure might mean to you (letting down teammates, end of career, etc.).
2. The 'physiological reaction to fear' that involves bodily changes, for example increased heart rate, more rapid breathing, sweaty palms, pale or flushed skin.
3. The 'behavioural response to fear', including fight mode disguised as anger where we might use physical strength to deal with the perceived threat; flight mode where our brain feels we cannot fight off the threat so it tries to escape; freeze mode where we go still, passive and quiet, hoping the threat will pass; fawn mode where the brain tries to go into people-pleasing mode to deal with the fear or threat.

These components are imperfectly linked, and it is possible to experience one or two without another. When you are your courageous self in fearful situations, you disconnect from the components of fear. You can be the witness or observer of your fears without getting overwhelmed by them. You realise that it is something happening within you, but it is not who you are.

Our bodies can have different chemical and mental reactions to fear that can feel uncomfortable, and we usually try to get rid of this discomfort as quickly as possible. We can become better at acknowledging this discomfort, accepting it as part of performing and allowing it to pass without trying to fight it, run from it or freeze because of it.

You accept some of the 'what if' scenarios. You acknowledge the unease in your body and realise it will pass if you stop resisting it. You make the decision to face that fearful situation despite the discomfort produced by your thoughts or your physical reactions.

How might this fear impact sports people negatively?

When getting ready to perform at any level, there is always evaluation. Our brain might be watching out for how spectators evaluate/view us, how our coaches evaluate/view us, how the opposition evaluate/view us and how teammates evaluate/view us. If we feel that these people's opinions matter to us then, of course, it is difficult not to be affected by how they view us, talk to us or even ignore us. If that teammate shames us for making a mistake, how will that impact how we think, feel and move in a game now or in the future? If a supporter criticises us, how will that impact us? If a coach frowns at us after a play, how might that impact us?

We can be impacted by negative feelings, such as fear, in multiple ways. Not feeling supported going into these uncertain situations can drive our system into a heightened state of fear. We can feel unable to communicate, we can feel lethargic and heavy, we can play with low-risk tolerance, we can be on the back foot straightaway. These are some of the avoidance behaviours that our fears can bring out in us.

When you are facing high-stakes situations that matter to you, it is normal for your fears to surface. The old limbic part of your brain scans for threats in your environment and it does this to keep you safe and protect you. This may have been very useful for our ancestors, but the 'danger' we experience today is more of an internal threat to our ego, reputation and perception. What will other people think of me? What will happen if I can't cope, if I fail in front of them?

The problem is that your body does not know the difference between internal and external threats and goes into protection mode to keep you safe. You can then experience different perceived feelings in your body that you can evaluate as negative – such as nerves versus excitement, thoughts that sound negative versus those that sound positive – and these can cloud your ability to think clearly and feel you are ready.

What are the sources of fear for you?

1. Does it come from expectation? Am I good enough or capable of delivering in this situation?
2. Does it come from the scrutiny of others, what they will think of me if I fail, for example family, friends, teammates, social media?
3. Does it come from the consequences of what will happen if I do fail, for example loss of role, loss of contract or career, selection?
4. Is this source of fear 100 per cent real or true? What part of it might be false? What evidence is there to suggest it is false most of the time? Is this belief irrational? Is this belief hurting my performance?
5. What is a new belief that I could replace this old belief with? This discomfort I am currently feeling means I am on the edge of moving out of my comfort zone and towards growth and greatness. I am capable and confident under pressure. I can learn and grow from failure.

So, what are some of the internal threats we can experience in the modern world? What do these fears feel like mentally and emotionally? Below are some of the internal fear responses you might recognise.

1. **The doubting self** Am I going to be good enough to perform at this level? I might begin to worry about my readiness for this experience. Will I be fit enough to last this? Will my pace get found out? My opponent is faster, stronger and more experienced than me. My attention and inner dialogue are very much on what I can't do and what I might not have in terms of skills. My self-talk is directed towards others and their capabilities rather than my own strengths and capabilities.
2. **The scared self** I need to get out of this situation. I might become very fearful of the outcome and not performing well in front of others. I might experience nausea. I am feeling very worried about what might happen in the future and the effect it will have on me. I am thinking worse-case scenario most of the time. I am creating a lot of 'what if' scenarios of what could go wrong. What if I mess up? What if I let my team down? What will my coaches think of me? How will my family feel if I crumble out there?
3. **The stressed self** Am I going to be okay in this situation? This feels tough sitting here waiting to perform. I am used to feeling tense about my matches. I am constantly thinking about the game and trying to distract myself with pre-game routines. My body feels warm and tight; I want to get out into the fresh air

and start the warm-up. I know I am using up energy but I am not quite sure how to control the stress.
4. **The panicked self** Unable to focus, distracted and overwhelmed. My stressed self has stepped over the threshold into panic. My legs or hands might be shaking. I am struggling to engage in what is happening around me. I am physically in the dressing room but am so caught up in my thoughts and bodily sensations that I can't take in any other information. I am running to the bathroom frequently. I can't tune in to what is being said or what I need to do now. My mind is racing.

At some point in your life, you may have started to believe your 'fear response' more than your voice of courage. The voice that said you will fail if you try something new, that you will feel shame and disappointment, that you are not good enough and that you are going to be found out sooner rather than later.

It is normal to be afraid of failing. Social media and society bombard us with judgement and comparison and tell us how we should think, feel and act. That our life, appearance and relationships need improvement. That this product or service will provide us with confidence or the feeling of being enough. There may be some deeper issues from childhood where the best-intentioned parent, teacher or coach thought they were helping you by giving you validation when you did something well but unintentionally ignored your feelings when you failed at something.

These feelings of inadequacy, of not measuring up to outside expectations, may come up whenever you fail at something, big or small. You may repeat these negative thoughts and feeling loops if you don't begin the work now.

But I do know this. Courage does not come from your genes, your upbringing, your education or social class. Courage is something we inherently have in different shapes and sizes. We express it in different ways. You are unique, interesting and special. You are born to express yourself, to express who you are and what you stand for.

Courage is not the absence of fear: it is being able to master your fear. You can do this in the following ways:

1. **Cognitively** How we think about our fears impacts how we feel and behave. Beware of the labels we attach to situations. Do we label important events as pressured or challenging, as exciting or anxiety-provoking? Do we see mistakes as something positive or negative? Are they something we can learn from? Do we think we need to be perfect in everything we do?
2. **Physiologically** How we move can lead to control or anxiety. If we are rushed, we will feel more anxious. Work on slowing your movements down. Slow down your walk between plays. Breathe more slowly.

I often get players to work on facing their fears by discussing these strategies with them prior to events. I use meditation to teach athletes how to access their relaxation response. When in this state of relaxation, I ask them to repeat words that they associate with this calm state on the inhale and exhale, for example, 'I am calm and present'. Breathing techniques will be discussed in depth in later chapters.

I then ask them to rehearse some of the possible scenarios they will face, using all their five senses. So, they will focus, for example, on mistakes that might happen, and they will learn how to deal with such scenarios through breathing or using a trigger word or action to restore their rhythm and flow, to enable them to move through this fear in a healthy way in a safe environment first.

Different types of fear require different types of courage. You might draw on your physical courage when lifting weights in a gym or making a strong tackle in a game. You might draw on your moral courage when discussing certain issues with your peers, where you might have opposing views. These could include politics, communication by your manager, or housing or health crises. This might be giving your point of view in a team video-analysis session. You may not want to look foolish in front of your peers, but your moral courage compels you to speak your truth.

What practices and exercises can you use to develop your inner courage, to help you to live a life with more courage? What might the most courageous version of you look, sound, feel and move like? What steps you can take to activate your inner courage?

1. You accept and welcome your stress or threat response. You become familiar with the thinking patterns of it, and you know that thoughts are not always facts and are not always truths. That the 'what if' scenario the mind is creating is just a story to keep you in your comfort zone. You can become familiar with the physical sensations of it. You observe those sensations

but know that feelings are not facts. You begin to observe your behavioural response. Is it to fight and resist the person or situation? Is it to freeze and become passive? Is it to take flight and flee the person or situation?
2. You decide on the new way you are going to think about this situation. Is this a challenge or a threat? A challenge perception might be: 'I am excited about this challenge. I know I have prepared well. I accept that not everything will go to plan. I focus on what I can control, my effort levels, my attention to the task and being present. The person I want to be in these situations is positive in terms of body language, words and actions. I am committed to helping my team. I am composed and finding the opportunities.'
3. You decide how to reframe the physical sensations you are feeling. This might sound like: 'My mind and body are getting excited to perform. With my adrenaline I am going to run faster, hit harder, go for longer and feel no pain.'
4. You decide to behave in a way that faces rather than avoids. You adopt the behaviours of the most courageous version of you. It is part of who you are now, and you take on new challenges at every opportunity. You put your chest out, head up, eyes looking forward and shoulders back. You breathe consciously through your nose. You get up on the balls of your feet. You act lively and alert. You communicate consistently. You take risks. You look for opportunities and demand the ball.

Exercise

FIND YOUR WHY

Knowing your *why* can help you act with purpose, which is your reason for being. It gives your life meaning, direction and inspiration. When you are doing something you love and that matters to you, you are generally at your best. You are in flow. Your *why* is born from past experiences, from your lessons learned and from values.

As German philosopher Frederich Nietzsche once said: 'He who has a *why* to live for can bear almost any *how*.' You must unlock your own *why* to overcome the fears your mind has created. And Simon Sinek's *Start with Why: How Great Leaders Inspire Everyone to Take Action* is a great resource to help you discover your why.

Below are examples of four questions, adapted from Dr Margie Warrell, to help you uncover why you do what you do. You can think about and write down your own responses to these questions.

1. **What makes you come alive on and off the field? What do you feel the most inspired and invigorated doing?**

   Being in the middle of a team pouring all my effort into helping us complete the task in front of us to a high standard. The love of preparing for new challenges and experiences. Going to places we haven't been before and conquering them internally as much as externally. Connecting with others at a deeper level through challenges, successes and setbacks.

2. **What are some of your innate strengths? Your superpowers that you feel give you an edge?**

   High levels of commitment to each task and desire to do things well. Communicate and connect well with others. Ability to learn quite quickly new methods and ways of operating. Can remain composed under pressure and bring high concentration levels to the task at hand.

3. **Where do you make the greatest contribution and impact on the teams you have been on?**

   Helping team members feel part of the group and reinforcing in them what they are extremely good at. Helping all group members feel valued and that their contribution matters. Being in the central positions on the field, encouraging and organising people to do their jobs to the best of their abilities. Helping people identify how we can improve and get better individually and collectively.

4. **What do you want your life to truly stand for? This is linked to your values from previous chapter.**

   To be an honest, kind and consistent person who did his best to be the best version of himself. To help make a positive impact on the world.

On the pitch

Over the past ten years working with teams, performance psychologist Gerry Hussey and I always put a huge emphasis on the mindset of 'love over fear'.

Love, at an energetic level, comes from the heart. Your heart emits an energy. It is said that this energy can reach up to eight feet around us. If you and your teammates are connected to a positive energy, it can affect the moods, energies and performances of individuals and the team as a whole. When you start operating more consistently from your heart, you radiate passion, positivity and enthusiasm.

Your brain and body produce positive chemicals like serotonin, oxytocin and dopamine that help you to feel calmer, more creative, more connected to others and more resilient. You are far more open to learning and growing. You are more likely to persist when things do not go to plan. You are more likely to take feedback as constructive rather than destructive. You are more likely to step into fear and face the situation.

We worked with several All-Ireland-winning GAA teams at club and county level. Some of the most important sessions we did with them were based on the mindset of love over fear. We would regularly sit players down in small groups and ask them to speak about why they were there. What did this team mean to them? Why did this matter to them beyond winning? What made this team special?

When the players spoke it very much centred around the love of each other, of family, of the team and the club. You could feel a powerful connection and bond forming in the room in those moments. People had to be vulnerable in front of forty of their peers. This vulnerability is not an easy thing to show, and it is not always modelled in society or sport. Men are meant to be mentally tough and are meant to show no weakness. Men are meant to keep their feelings to themselves. It takes courage to speak from your heart and to show sides of you that no one has seen before.

This ability to be vulnerable built huge trust and respect in the group. When any member was going through difficult times on or off the field, they had this blanket of support around them.

It took us all through many difficult moments. One player spoke about the promise he made to his dad before he died that he would win an All-Ireland medal for him. That there was no way he was going to let his father down and break his promise. How he wanted the love, commitment and support of everyone in the team to make it happen. He was also respectful of every player and their motives to succeed.

Another player spoke about how if someone made a mistake in a game, no one in the group would think any less of them as a person. 'There is a no-blame culture here,' he said. This gave the group the psychological safety to admit and make mistakes. There would be no shaming there.

These moments of love and connection between the players created enormous shifts in trust. It enabled people to be truly authentic in expressing their truths about who they are, what matters to them and their view of the world. It enabled them to express their deepest strengths as people, on and off the field. It enabled them to detach from the societal pressures of 'fitting in' or 'following the crowd', thereby avoiding the discomfort of failing at something over fear of shame, embarrassment or ridicule.

Summary

In this chapter, I introduced to you the idea that courage versus fear is one of the challenges you will meet. That without some level of healthy fear, you cannot access courage. Your fear response is not a bad thing; it is there to protect you and keep you safe. To access your courage muscle, it is necessary to experience fear, to take on exciting challenges where success is uncertain.

To embrace challenges and conquer them, you must first understand how your mind, body and behaviours respond to fear. Your fear tends to come from your expectations ('Am I good enough?'), judgements ('What will others think if I fail?') and consequences ('What will happen if I fail?'). When you redefine what these sources mean to you, you redefine your relationship to fear. Fear helps you to grow and develop; it enables you to understand your comfort zone and where you can stretch the perceived limits of your capabilities. It enables you to access levels of courage that you never believed you had.

When you start to feel fear, redefine the source that affects you, and reinterpret the physical sensations as your mind and body prepare for an exciting performance. Focus on the person you are (your values) rather than the outcome. You will start to walk towards these opportunities on a frequent basis, loving the challenge and the excitement flowing through you.

Love and fear cannot coexist. By focusing on love, you dilute the negative thinking, feelings and behaviours presented by fear.

When you are clear about what you want to achieve (your goals), why those goals matter to you (your why/purpose) and how you want to achieve them (your values), you have focused your perspective on love.

Love overpowers fear all the time. Focus on what matters to you. Focus on the person you want to be. Focus on approaching situations with love and passion – then watch your courage, meaning and convictions grow.

3

OUTCOME VERSUS PROCESS

IN LIFE AND SPORT, WE OFTEN HEAR THAT A PERSON or team is very motivated or driven. What does that mean? What does a driven or motivated person look and sound like? Do people who are perceived to be high performers feel motivated constantly?

We can explore this by looking at two approaches to the same situation, one from an *outcome* mindset and the other from a *process* one.

When I am focused on the 'outcome' of a situation, my goal becomes about demonstrating that my ability is the same or better than others. Success and achievement are realised when I reach a desired outcome, such as winning a major competition, which involves outperforming others. This athlete is extrinsically motivated and can feel pressure as they compare their performances and outcomes to those of others. They can put unhelpful expectations on themselves ('I need to win this competition'). When they don't live up to these expectations, their self-esteem can be affected, they can feel a lack of control in terms of their development and they can become less engaged in their chosen sport.

When I am constantly in this outcome-focused mindset and putting my energy and attention into being better than others, I can lose sight of the progress I am making, what I am learning in the gym or how I'm preparing for games. I feel a constant pressure, as the only success for me is in winning, in trying to be better than others. If I only have a competition or a game every couple of weeks, will I only feel fulfilment for one or two hours a month if I succeed in that 'outcome only' mindset game?

When I am focused on the 'process' of completing a task, such as lifting my heaviest squat or beating my previous best in the gym, the goal is to develop mastery of my squat technique, to improve on my previous best or to identify any limitation in my technique or if my mindset is hindering my approach. Success and the feeling of achievement is realised when mastery of the task occurs or when improvement happens during the process of the lift.

The reward is in the effort put in and what has been mastered in my approach, improved on from my previous standard and learned from doing the task or implementing the process to the best of my ability. I am doing this task for my own sense of accomplishment rather than trying to please or gain approval from an external source, be it a coach, manager or parent.

This might be referred to as the intrinsically motivated athlete. These athletes focus on the betterment of themselves or the team rather than a constant focus on individual accolades or winning trophies. This enables them to focus more on the present moment, on what they can control, and it reduces self-judgement or harsh comparison to others, which can lower self-esteem. With this process-oriented thinking, athletes feel more in control, can manage their emotions better, have higher self-esteem, can persevere longer, can engage in learning longer and can produce more consistent improvements over time.

The team environment around you also plays a critical role in this outcome-versus-process focus. If coaches and players define success only by results, by being better than other teams or individuals, this can create an unhealthy environment where worry about failing becomes constant. Consequently, people might avoid challenging tasks or getting feedback out of fear of embarrassment, and the ambition of athletes can be reduced when social comparison with others' ability is the dominant metric of success.

Both coaches and athletes have a responsibility to set healthy expectations for success – expectations that are more grounded in individual and team standards of performance rather than constant comparison to other athletes or teams. This process-orientated focus helps us to get more enjoyment, participation and progression throughout our sporting journeys.

My journey to the process mindset

When I think of my younger self preparing for big games and national finals from 2000 to 2006, I think of an inexperienced, uncertain and worried person. I was approaching the biggest games in my career with very little awareness of my motivational approach – I didn't have a clear vision of the player I wanted to be.

I didn't know fully why I was playing for Galway. I was not clear on who I was or what I stood for. I did not really understand what made me able to compete at that level. I did not really understand what helped me to be in the best mental, physical, technical and tactical shape for these important situations. I was very much in an outcome-oriented thinking process, comparing my standards to others, judging myself critically when I wasn't achieving success instantly and having quite low self-esteem most of the time.

It was when we were exposed to a sport psychologist John McGuire for the first time in 2006 that I began to look at some of these important questions around motivation, preparation and performance.

In our first session, I told him how I had felt during the 2005 season when approaching big games, including the All-Ireland final, and how I struggled with anxiety around my performances. This anxiety was coming from the fear of letting down other people – my teammates, family and friends.

I had a fear of not performing as well as I had in my last game. A fear of losing. These fears were inhibiting my preparation and performances. I would be regularly running to the toilet for two to three hours before a big game. I had no idea at that stage what hidden expectations I had of myself, apart from winning and playing well. I had no definition of what playing well looked like, and what I was referencing as a good performance was just comparison with others and how they did versus how I did.

These comparisons could be happening before the game in terms of negative self-talk, for example about being not experienced enough to mark Brian Corcoran, the Cork full-forward in that 2005 All-Ireland final. They could come during the game when judging how many balls I lost to my opponent or how many scores I had conceded.

Over a couple of sessions, John helped me to identify what I looked like, sounded like and felt like when I was at my best. What actions enabled me to excel in games.

In the 2006 season, I began to use a notebook for the first time to become process-oriented in my thinking, feeling and doing. I would write down key goals for myself each day. I would plan out my meals, training and recovery. These helped me to remain present and focused on the daily task at hand, rather than worrying about the big game at the weekend. They helped me to recognise when I was focusing on things that were outside my control.

I identified what my strengths were as a player, and I began to work on these in training. I began to visualise myself doing these things in championship matches as John had taught me. We had a visualisation session before most games, which would help me to identify how I was going to play, and I would rehearse the key moves over and over in my mind.

I began to work on my self-talk throughout the day. I used daily affirmations to build my self-image and belief in myself. I had learned these from many of Bob Rotella's books, such as *Your 15th Club*, and had adapted them for my own approach. I found these affirmations so powerful in changing how I viewed myself. For many years, at senior level, I had told myself that I was not fast enough or not good enough, and when I played poorly it just strengthened that belief. When you have told yourself this for several seasons, you start to believe it as fully factual and completely true. You disregard any previous accomplishments, and when you have one good display, you start thinking immediately that you will get found out in your next display.

I had a lot of work to do on my self-image as a hurler, so I worked daily on my affirmations and started to visualise myself doing the things I knew I could do. Over time, I began to recognise my strengths more consistently. I began to speak to myself in a much more positive and helpful way when approaching important moments in training and games. I would repeat statements with energy and emotion: 'I am strong, powerful and confident.' As a result, I felt less stressed going into games. I felt more focused daily. I spent more of my time and energy preparing for the things I could control.

I now had a clearly defined process for my training, preparation and matches. There was more consistency in my preparation, and I felt confident and focused for games. I began to love the process mindset of learning and improving. My whole perception and outlook had shifted from outcome, from comparison and from judgement. I felt real freedom playing games that season.

Moving from having vague outcome-focused goals to a process-led approach made a huge difference to my enjoyment of training, preparation and matches.

Recognising negative mindsets (and why we have them)

Why do we become so focused on outcomes? We are all naturally competitive on some level. It can feel good from a sports perspective to beat an opponent to a ball or to score a match-winning goal. This can give us a boost in self-esteem, mood and motivation to repeat similar feats again. Of course, there can be healthy competition that drives us to put in more effort, improve our skills or show our desire to win the ball by sprinting harder than an opponent. Competition becomes unhealthy when we constantly feel pressure to be better than someone, when we physically hurt someone intentionally to beat them or when we feel we are never enough for our parents or coaches, even when we win.

We can become attached to the idea that we will feel great when we win and feel like a failure when we lose. This is our mind and body playing games with us.

Unfortunately, a lot of society is focused on results. We are graded at a young age in school as intelligent or not. We get approval for our grades from teachers, parents, peers and the culture we live in. We are given points for our Leaving Certificate and told what colleges and course we can attend. We are measured in sport and often graded on A, B or C teams as talented or less talented. It can be hard, therefore, to avoid having a total outcome focus when society seems to validate or vindicate us for achievement in these areas.

It can become part of our self-identity that we get approval when we do well academically, so we keep striving for more and more qualifications to feel approved by society. When we do well in sport we can get approval from others too, so we strive for more and more success.

We then realise when we get to the workplace that our IQ (intelligence) is only a small part of being successful in our careers, and that it is more important to have EQ (emotional intelligence). Skills like self-awareness, self-confidence and self-control are vital in leading ourselves. Skills like straightforward communication, relationship skills and empathy are critical in leading others. Skills like adaptability, optimism and self-actualisation are important in our ever-changing and complex environment. You may not have been taught these skills during your time in education, and so you must learn them for yourself in order to become a better leader in your workplace, in your sports team and in your community.

Ego

To understand how we can become attached to outcomes, we must speak about our ego. Our ego is a part of all our personalities. It is an individual's sense of self-esteem or self-worth. It is the way someone views or perceives themselves – their self-awareness.

Ego is a spectrum. It's neither good nor bad, it's a matter of degree or context. Positive aspects include confidence, security of identity and self-belief. Negative aspects are attributed to criticism of self and others, needing approval and the need to feel superior.

Ego can be a powerful driver of performance when used in the right way. Think of an athlete like Ronaldo; he has a high degree of self-confidence, and this healthy sense of self enables him to consistently perform on the biggest occasions. He has a drive and a desire to be the best soccer player ever to have played the game. He might be perceived by others as arrogant but, for me, he has a high degree of humility in realising the hard work he needs to do off the field in terms of lifestyle, gym and recovery. He is said to be one the hardest-working athletes ever in soccer. He recognises he is not the finished product and constantly strives to improve himself. His ego does seem to like the acclaim of being the best player in the world and his ambition is to win individual awards, like the Ballon d'Or (which we could argue is an outcome focus). I would bet he does set these outcome goals for himself each year, but he is very much process-focused in his thinking and actions on improving day-to-day and helping the team to improve, which he recognises is fundamental to his success too. He has good morals in terms of his respect for his family, his charity work and being a role model in promoting soccer worldwide.

The unhealthy side to our egos is when we become self-centred or self-focused. We have an inflated sense of self-confidence, and having success can feed into this sense of self-importance. We can become arrogant, not considerate of our teammates' roles, perhaps do not listen and belittle others to feed our arrogance.

The role of ego in our performance

Most of us derive who we are from our thoughts and from the stories we tell ourselves repeatedly throughout our day.

Your ego first identifies with your possessions; as a child this may have been your first toy and when this was taken from you, you felt pain and you possibly shouted and screamed. Your ego mind had identified this possession as yours. As you advance through life your story and your thoughts expand into your relationships ('these are people I like/dislike'), your ability ('I am talented at this'), your knowledge in a particular area, your sports team or your sport.

If someone has a different opinion to you about these things your ego mind can become defensive, upset, aggressive and fearful. You think these thoughts/stories are who you are, for example your self-image or self-identity. So, you try to defend them with all your might.

If, as a young person, I feel accepted for being good at sport, for being strong academically or for my physical appearance, this is what I will work hard to protect and defend when my ego is at play. The healthy side of this is the ambition and drive you might have to do well at sport, achieve academically or to stay healthy. The unhealthy side is when we have a limited view of ourselves only as a 'sports person' or as a student 'academic'. Then, when we don't do well or achieve external validation in this area, our sense of self-worth is impacted. We might feel shame, embarrassment or a lack of self-worth.

So, in sport for example, when we begin to fail at something or don't perform as we wanted to, our ego tends to put down others to protect ourselves from our own pain, and this, of course, can cause issues with our teammates, coaches or opponents. Our ego can prevent us from moving out of our comfort zone in case we get exposed as not being good enough. Our ego, in trying to protect us, might not want feedback on our game as it is too painful to hear that we have flaws and limitations in some areas. Of course, these defence mechanisms are not protecting us: they are holding us back from finding the next level of our authentic self.

Sometimes, the ego protects us in hidden ways that are hard to detect. We may not be aware that we compare ourselves to people who are not on the same path as us. For example, why don't I have as much speed or success as Ronaldo? This is not a good comparison when we consider the number of resources and the level of experience Ronaldo has in professional environments.

We may not be aware of the thoughts we are having in relation to ourselves, other people and the world, and how these stories are impacting our present and our future. If we are unaware or unconscious, we can default to the negative side of our ego. We are then in comparison, judgement and defence mode, and it can be hard to make the necessary changes to get closer to our potential.

Another thing we must remember is that the ego is always in seeking mode. It is never satisfied. It will never be enough or have enough. It is always lacking, be it sport skills, success, money, knowledge, appearance, career status or relationships. The future is all-important to it. This can give sports people the drive to keep improving and wanting more but it can be unhealthy in terms of never reaching happiness, fulfilment or success, regardless of your achievements to date.

This is why living in the now in process-orientated thinking helps us to move away from an ego outcome focus of seeking more and more, not feeling enough or worthy despite what you do and the future being all-important.

The goal is to recognise that we all have these tendencies. That our ego will be with us on the journey. We must be aware of it and ensure that we are doing things that make us happy, that matter to us, and ensure that we are seeking out the right successes for our own internal joy and mastery, rather than seeking validation or approval from others to be enough or feel worthy of love or acceptance.

Feeling overwhelmed

When you get overly focused on the outcome approach to goals, you start to become more anxious, overwhelmed and panicked around specific events. Why does this happen? In this world, it is going to be extremely hard to be better than seven billion people at any one thing. The ego mind can put us into threat state, and we can start to feel unsafe, insecure and uncertain when in situations where judgement and opinion are inevitable.

With an outcome focus, how might our ego react to all these eyes watching us? We can feel nervous, anxious and worried – none of which will help us access our best self.

It is not that these outcome goals are bad and don't work to some extent, but, from my experience, when you are trying to deal with long-term, high-pressure situations and high performance, outcome goals put unnecessary pressure on the individual. They can take away the enjoyment of your sport when too much emphasis is placed on them. They are, for the most part, not in your control.

As humans we like to feel we have a level of influence and control over our destiny. Outcomes can increase pressure on athletes to perform and can impact their self-esteem. Do you think that waiting for longer term success will make you happier than you have ever been? Will you continue to enjoy the process, identify progress, recognise the memories and experiences that you are having, identify the values that you are developing around teamwork, connection, commitment, resilience and learning if you are entirely focused on how your ability compares to others?

I have spent full seasons of my sporting career worrying about outcomes rather than enjoying the process. It is important to set these outcome goals to give direction, but when I was overly outcome-focused, it impacted my enjoyment of hurling in a very negative way. When I wasn't starting at number six in a training game, my ego mind would default to negativity mode. I would get caught up in my 'inner worrier', again based on harsh judgement and criticism. 'Management must not rate me. They obviously think he is better.' When I had a bad game in league or championship my 'inner worrier' would start telling me that I would never get an All-Star. If I wasn't picked for a league game, the 'inner worrier' would tell me the manager was ruining my chances of winning an All-Star and All-Ireland. This was my ego mind in a threat state, worrying about my position on the team, worrying would I be good enough. It was trying to protect me and keep me safe from the pain of not being enough.

Mental training

Establish your motivation process

To help you move away from having a solely outcome-focused approach to goals, it is important to examine your motivational approach to challenges.

Motivation is about the intensity and direction of your actions. The clearer you are in understanding what direction you want to go, the more your energy and intensity will follow. You face many choices and distractions daily. Knowing what you want, and why, and having a plan to achieve it can increase your chances of completing these goals by up to 75 per cent.

It is in your nature to want and strive for the things you deem valuable in life. Motivation gives you insight about what you truly care about and why you want certain things – be that success, happiness or health. Your motivation reflects something unique about you and can help you improve your performance, health, well-being and sense of purpose.

A simple process can help identify our needs and wants.

1. Establish what you truly care about. For example, health, relationships, career, adventure, contribution, education, financial independence.
2. What do you enjoy most doing? For example, playing sport, sea swimming, seeing new places, learning.
3. What gives you energy? For example, exercising, being out in nature, spending time with close friends, watching something you enjoy.

4. Identify goals for each area of your life that matters to you, as per number 1 above. What would you like to be true in that area in the short term (one month), medium term (three to six months) and long term (nine to twelve months)?

When you have identified your needs and wants, you can use a goal-setting framework to set goals, like SMARTCAR.

Specific What is the specific goal you want to achieve in your health, career, relationships, etc?

Measurable How would you know you have achieved it?

Action-related What are the specific actions you can take today and this week to move you forward?

Realistic Is the goal realistic for you to achieve?

Timed What date do you expect to complete the goal by?

Commitment How committed are you on a scale of 0 to 100 per cent of achieving this goal?

Accountability Who could you tell your goal and plan to? Who could help with the goal, plan and accountability?

Rewards What are the benefits of achieving this goal? List as many as you can.

5. What is your process (some daily actions you can do) to grow and nourish these areas now and move you closer to your short-, medium- and long-term goals?

By identifying your true needs and wants – and setting goals around them – your motivation becomes clearer, enabling you to improve your thinking, feeling and, ultimately, behaviours.

When you approach situations with positive thoughts, feelings and behaviours, it empowers you to grow your skills, be goal-oriented, be creative, make plans, be engaged and purposeful with your actions, progress quicker and achieve more.

Motivation can be defined as the drive to take part in and persist at an activity. There are several content and process theories of motivation. For this chapter, I am mostly focusing on elements of achievement motivation. There are three components to motivation.

- **Direction** Where you direct your efforts, for example choosing one activity over another. Today, you choose to do a running session over a gym session as you want to work on aerobic fitness rather than strength.
- **Persistence** Continuing with an activity until you have completed it. You set yourself the goal of jogging for forty-five minutes today. You are feeling tired at forty minutes, but you continue and persist to hit your training goal of forty-five minutes.
- **Intensity** The amount of energy you devote to that activity. Your low-intensity jog for forty-five minutes will not require as much intensity as a short, repeated sprint session with skills thrown in.

It is important when speaking about motivation that we are aware of internal factors and external factors that help with our direction, persistence and intensity.

There are two main types of motivation – intrinsic motivation and extrinsic motivation.

- **Intrinsic motivation** relates to the internal factors, such as the enjoyment you get from mastering skills, or from being stimulated and challenged.
- **Extrinsic motivation** relates to external factors, the rewards you get from doing an activity, for example praise from others, status, fame, trophies, medals.

The perspective on motivation I like to use with athletes is a mix of outcome-focused goals where we set high expectations for ourselves in terms of wanting to reach a particular destination. We have the mental intention to be an All-Ireland winner, European champion or world champion and we look at the outcome goals along the way to winning these titles (be it winning pre-season competitions, league or group stages of championships). The second part then is to look at our day-to-day motivation in terms of task or process goals to reach our outcome goals along the way. This is about falling in love with the journey and identifying the key technical, tactical, mental, physical and lifestyle skills it will take to be that champion. We can then put most of our energy and attention into the controllable and specific tasks that will help us develop into that champion. This gives the person a sense of control and responsibility in reaching their destination and they can see the improvements they are making along the journey, which nourishes their motivation to stay on the process and task more frequently. The type of motivation that you use can have a correlation with a process-oriented mindset or goals-oriented mindset.

The good news is that you are not fixed as someone who has an outcome or a process focus. You can change.

You can look at your process and see what you learned from failing. You can adjust to have more success the next time. Success is never the end of the journey and failure is never fatal. There will always be new goals and ambitions to go after.

Exercises

EXERCISE 1: CURRENT REALITY ON OUTCOME VERSUS PROCESS

To move your focus from the outcome approach, you must first identify your current behaviours. Reflect on whether during tasks you take the process approach or outcome approach by using the table below.

PROCESS APPROACH	OUTCOME APPROACH
Prefer challenging tasks	Avoid challenging tasks for fear of looking incompetent

PROCESS APPROACH	OUTCOME APPROACH
Focus on task mastery (learning, understanding), improving competencies	Focus on demonstrating competence over others
Belief that learning/growth happens at different rates for different people	Belief that learning/growth happens quickly or not at all
Base satisfaction on effort exerted	Base satisfaction on outcomes achieved
Increase effort if setback happens	Decrease effort if setback happens
Attribute failure to lack of effort	Attribute failure to lack of ability
Engage in consistent self-monitoring	Stick to what I am good at as it is 'safe' and I know that I am good at it

EXERCISE 2: BUILDING YOUR PLAN TO GET THERE

In order to move more towards a process approach, you need to develop a process and performance plan. It is important to include your outcome goals so you have a destination in mind, though this should be about 1 per cent of your emphasis each time you set goals for training, game, competition or season.

Be clear on the outcome – the person you want to be or the outcome you want to achieve is the first step.

The second step is being clear on the process, such as the tasks and behaviours necessary to achieve that outcome. Your focus should be on this 99 per cent of the time as you move through your day, training session or competition.

The goal is to master your process, and the outcomes will take care of themselves. For each of the bullet points below, write down how these items relate to your own personal journey.

- **Person** The type of person I am or want to become, e.g. honest, positive or relentless (as covered in Chapter 1).
- **Process** Goals that will help with consistency in preparation and training. The tasks and behaviour processes that will help me achieve my performance goals, e.g. sleeping enough, eating healthily or attending all the training sessions. The key here is actions that are positive, specific to your role and controllable to enable you to achieve your performance goals.
- **Performance** Goals that I want to be consistent on in-game. The match-day goals I set to help achieve my outcome goals. Usually based on the previous performance or previous best performance, e.g. number of tackles completed, passes completed or shots converted.
- **Outcome goals** Setting new performance goals from previous standards, e.g. making a team, winning the game, winning individual awards or winning team competitions.
- Review process and progress.

When you have indicated your own personal processes, performances and outcome goals, it is helpful to categorise these into three phases:

- **Preparation phase** Non-negotiables: your day-to-day tasks and behaviours.
- **Peformance phase** During training or in-game.
- **Review phase** Reflection after a training session, match, league season, etc.

The below table will help you to set out your own process and performance plan.

PREPARATION PHASE
NON-NEGOTIABLES

AREA	PROCESS	OUTCOME
Sleep	• Get off devices 30 minutes before going to sleep. • Do 10 pages of light reading. • Do 10 sets of light breathing exercises (inhale through the nose for 4 seconds, pause at top of breath for 4 seconds, exhale through nose or mouth for 4 seconds, rest for 4 seconds and repeat 10 times).	To achieve eight hours of deep, restful sleep.
Meditation	• On waking, have earphones by the bed. • Switch on guided meditation video from YouTube or an app.	To do 20 minutes daily to achieve greater emotional stability and awareness.

AREA	PROCESS	OUTCOME
Nutrition	• Start the day with healthy breakfast, for example porridge, smoothie and different supplements that might be required like fish oils, multivitamins, etc. • Consistent non-processed food every 3 hours. • Light and healthy snacks between main meals.	• To feel energised, enthusiastic and recovered. • 5–10g per kg of body weight for carbs amount, 0.75g of proteins per kg of body weight and 0.5–1.5g fats per kg of body weight for training/non-training days.
Movement	• Spend time each day moving the body, gym work, walking, running, yoga or field-based session. • Spend at least 15 to 30 minutes in daylight in the morning and as the sun goes down in the evening.	• To release positive chemicals into the mind/body. • To do 30 minutes daily of low-intensity walking for active recovery.
Journalling	• Spend time on planning what key tasks you are committed to doing to grow your health, relationships, career, contribute to your community, etc. • Reflect on what you enjoyed from your daily experiences. • Reflect on small or big successes you had and what you are grateful for.	• To grow and recognise our strengths, what we learned, what we have and the person we want to be. • To journal for 5 to 10 minutes each day.

PERFORMANCE PHASE
PROCESS + PERFORMANCE = OUTCOME

PROCESS (TASK/ACTION RELATED GOALS)	PERFORMANCE	OUTCOME
1. Get my head up quickly in possession. 2. Scan left and right, in front and inside. 3. Decide and execute.	• If I get 10 possessions in a game, I want to execute 8 to 10 accurate passes.	To be a composed player in possession by hitting over 80 per cent accurate passes.
1. Stand tall, chest out, shoulders back, head up, eyes looking forward not down. 2. Direct my attention to the task and positive cue words. 3. Communicate with teammates consistently on our positioning and roles.	• Every opportunity to be a radiator of energy, not a drain. • Bring positive energy to the group and the moment. • Organise my defence through clear and specific instructions.	To be a positive communicator in body language and words.
1. Be active on the balls of my feet. Be aggressive in 50/50 contests on the ground, in the air and in the tackle. 2. Demand the ball when available. 3. Move into space to support runs to help teammates.	• Aim to win 80 per cent of the contests with my opponent. • Aim to get on 15-plus possessions to help the team. • Aim to get on 5 short puckouts to start attacks.	To be relentless in playing to win.

REVIEW PHASE
REFLECT AND LEARN

Preparation What habits helped me to feel prepared, energised and confident this week?
Preparation What one thing would I change from my preparation this week that would make the biggest difference to my performance next week?
Process What worked well from my process goals? What one thing will I improve this week and how?
Performance How did I do in relation to my performance goals? What progress did I make? Where can I grow and how?
Lesson What was I most proud of over the past week? Where and when did I feel most motivated to achieve success? What was I thinking, feeling and doing?

On the pitch

In his book *The Real McCaw*, All Black captain Richie McCaw tells the story of setting his vision and goals as a twelve-year-old as he sat with his grandfather in a café in New Zealand.

His grandfather asked him what his dream in life was and Richie said he wanted to be an All Black. His grandfather pushed him some more, saying there have been lots of All Black players over the past 100-plus years, why would you want to be just an All Black?

He then gave his grandson a napkin and biro and asked him to write down how he would become an All Black. So, Richie wrote down the teams he would be playing for and when – when he would make different underage club, provincial and All Black teams and when he would make his debut for the seniors.

Then, his grandfather asked him to write down what type of All Black he would like to be remembered as. Young Richie hesitantly wrote that he wanted to be a great All Black.

With that, he had set out the first two pieces around his vision and purpose. From that day on, Richie trained, prepared and performed in every game to create that 'great All Black'. He made his senior debut two years ahead of his prediction and ended his career with 131 wins from 148 test games. He became one of the most successful and respected players of all time, winning three World Player of the Year awards and captaining New Zealand to two World Cups.

The identity and process that accelerated his success were as follows.

The person he wanted to be was *respectful*. He wanted to go out and perform because he wanted to earn the respect of the guys he played with. He wanted to inspire them by his actions. He wanted his opponents to know they were going to be challenged in every way.

He wanted *commitment* to the process and to have *honest* conversations between coaches and players when those standards of preparation and performance were not met.

He wanted to *trust* his teammates to do their jobs and had high expectations of them.

He wanted to be *consistent* and do the basics brilliantly.

He wanted to be *composed*, moving from the 'red head', where he can be off-task and panicking, to the 'blue head' that is on-task and in control. The red head and blue head are a method the All Blacks used to recognise when they had lost emotional control in pressure situations. The red head is when people become disconnected from the present moment and become fixated on the past or future. The blue head is when people are in the present moment, clear and focused on the specific task at hand.

In his quest to be a great All Black, Richie McCaw focused on the task at hand every single day. He respected the privilege and honour of wearing the jersey. He knew the huge levels of preparation required and the mindset he needed as he approached each game.

So, Richie's approach to being a great All Black was grounded in values like being respectful, trusting and committed. He placed huge emphasis on a process to achieving these outcome goals for himself and the team.

Summary

When you move your motivational approach from overly outcome-focused measures to more process-focused measures, you will feel more in control, excited and less fearful. You will begin to open yourself to real growth and expansion. You will not be limiting yourself to just one measure of success to motivate you and will begin to see the unique opportunities for growth in each experience and recognise the competencies you have built during the process of preparing for it. You will begin to appreciate the strengths you have harnessed even further by stretching yourself in your performance domain. You will see the journey of learning, growing and discovering as hugely satisfying, and you will begin to approach situations with passion, love and curiosity, and reduce the negative side of trying to avoid failure.

The shift to feeling in control of your success enables you to move from anxiety and panic to excitement and readiness. By identifying clearly your internal and external motives for success, you can begin to see the patterns that are unhelpful to your performance and the factors that support a motivated, driven and decisive person.

4

THREAT VERSUS CHALLENGE

WHEN YOU ARE FACING DIFFICULT SITUATIONS IN life, how do your mind and body react? How do they react when you believe you can be successful? How do they react when you believe you will fail?

Blascovich's biopsychosocial model of challenge and threat, revised by Meijen *et al.* (2020), suggests that, prior to a task such as a sporting competition, an athlete will make an evaluation of the demands they are likely to encounter and whether they have the resources to cope (see figure on page 91).

Your mind and body respond to pressure in two ways – one is helpful for performance; the other can hinder it. These two responses are the *challenge* and the *threat* states. When you approach pressure situations in a challenge state, you are more likely to perform well. When you approach them in a threat state, you are more likely to perform poorly.

CHALLENGE STATE BEHAVIOURS	THREAT STATE BEHAVIOURS
Dominant	Submissive
Confident	Unconfident
Composed	On edge
Focused	Unfocused
Challenged	Threatened
Accurate	Inaccurate

When an athlete is in a challenge state, they respond positively to any stress. They are focused on what can be gained from a potentially stressful scenario and they believe they have the resources to cope with the stress.

A threat state, on the other hand, embodies a negative mental approach to pressure, where the athlete's mental resources do not meet the demands of the situation. They are more focused on what could go wrong and do not believe they have the resources to cope with the stress.

There are physiological changes that happen when we are in challenge state – we produce a stronger cardiac output, we release

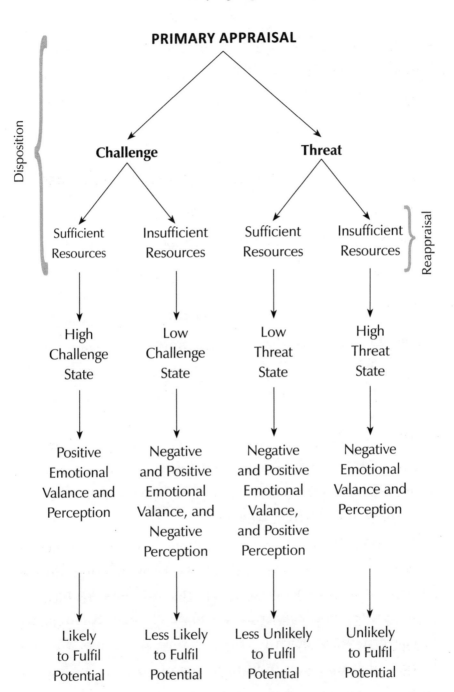

fatty acids, which can be used as fuel by the brain and muscles, and blood flow to those areas is increased – and it is these physiological changes that help us cope quickly with any stress. When in a threat state, there is an increase in blood pressure levels – blood flow is restricted, so our ability to make decisions and to move slows down. Fatty acids are converted over a longer period, which is not conducive to coping with stress.

Some interesting non-verbal implications were seen in a study by Brimmell *et al.* (2018), who looked at different non-verbal behaviours of soccer players during a pressurised penalty task.

Those athletes who demonstrated dominance, confidence, composure, focus, challenge and performance accuracy were the ones who evaluated the penalty task as a challenge, while the athletes who saw the task as a threat had more negative behaviours.

My journey to the challenge state

In the 2012 Leinster hurling final, Galway faced Kilkenny, a team that had won eight All-Irelands since 2000. I had never beaten them in a national final before at any level, and this was on my mind briefly in the lead-up to the game. We all felt that the past was not something we'd could change, and winning the first Leinster title for our county was a goal we all had since November 2011 when we sat down for the first time as a group. We fully believed that we had it in us to be successful that day. It was a highly relevant goal for us to achieve.

The second assessment of the game in front of us was on the demands we would face. There was going to be some physical danger in our environment because of the physicality in how Kilkenny played. We knew we were well prepared for the intensity of that battle, through our in-house training games and our league and championship games so far.

There was low danger to our esteem as a group because no one from inside or outside our county expected us to succeed. This helped take the pressure from us. We were confident in our abilities and that we would perform but, of course, the result was out of our control. We needed to focus on what we could control in terms of our skills and resources.

We absolutely knew it was going to need a huge mental and physical effort to be successful. Our thought process from the outset was about focusing on ourselves, our attitude, game plan and performance, which helped us move away from the outcome focus and social comparison with Kilkenny and their history, successes and abilities.

We had a high perceived control of our skills, as we focused on our controllable performance measures, such as our high intensity, discipline in tackling and supporting one another in each situation.

We had a high focus on 'approach goals' (playing to succeed rather than to avoid failing), by concentrating on playing to win the ball in our area, working hard and making the best decisions for the team.

We had a high perception of social support within the group, that no matter what happened on the field, we would encourage and back each other up throughout the match. We were in this together. Everyone could make a mistake; it is how we responded to the next ball that mattered.

There was a very positive feeling in the group that day, and we knew that we were ready for the battle. We did feel some nerves at different stages of the build-up and in the game, but we interpreted this as our minds and bodies getting ready to perform – we saw nerves more as an excited feeling rather than something that shouldn't be happening to us. This reframing of nerves to excitement was helpful and would enhance our performance. We were doing something we cared deeply about and for a team we cared deeply about.

Yes, we made lots of mistakes that day by giving away some poor scores and making some poor decisions at times, but we had worked hard all year to respond to setbacks with positive action or intention.

Being in this challenge state enabled our team to fulfil its potential that day. We remained in the challenge state leading up to and during the game by focusing on what we believed we were good at and the skills we had to perform to a high standard.

We remained focused on the things we could control, such as our attitude, effort and behaviours, and we broke the game down into smaller tasks. All these factors enabled us to be in a challenge state more consistently and to remain process focused throughout.

The outcome was that we beat Kilkenny by 2–21 to 2–11 in a very controlled and dominant performance. Because of how we viewed ourselves, the opposition and the challenge, we were in a high challenge state for most of the match. Our minds and bodies responded with efficient energy and resources, and we had better decision-making, emotional control, attention control and physical movement.

Recognising negative mindsets

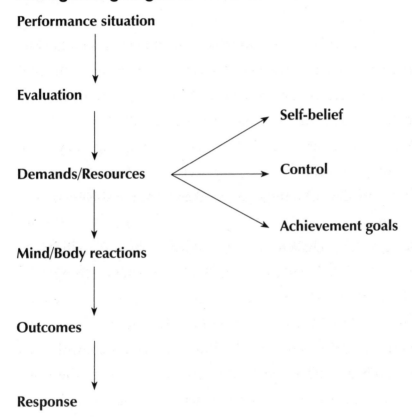

What are the factors most associated with the challenge and threat states, and how do they affect us?

The above graphic is what occurs mentally when you face a performance situation. First you complete a quick evaluation:

'Can I cope with this stress, yes or no'. Then, you begin to evaluate the physical effort required to deal with the situation and, finally, the mental effort. These are called the demands. You then evaluate the resources you have to cope with these demands. These determine whether you will experience a challenge or a threat state. These are control, self-efficacy and your achievement goal perspective.

Athletes who experience challenge states have greater attentional control compared to those in a threat state – so they can maintain their focus on the target better.

Self-efficacy refers to a person's belief in their ability to be successful. The higher this is, the better they feel they can cope in stressful situations.

Using tools, like focusing on past positive accomplishments and experiences, can help you achieve success. Using techniques, like visualising the performance you want, rehearsing the challenges you will encounter and having a plan to cope with these stressful moments, can help with challenge states.

The type of goals you set can have a bearing on whether you experience a challenge or threat state.

There are four types of goals we can set according to Elliot and McGregor's (2001) 2x2 achievement goal model:

- **Mastery-approach goals** These are where you strive to perform better than your previous performance or personal best. They are more positively associated with challenge states in athletes. Your achievements are self-referenced, and you are focused on improving your own standards of performance.

- **Mastery-avoidance goals** These are where you strive not to do worse than a previous performance. The goals are still self-referenced but are negative in nature.
- **Performance-approach goals** These are where you are focused on performing better than an opponent in a match or a teammate in training. They are negative in the sense that the athlete is trying to avoid performing worse than a specific standard. These performance goals are associated with both challenge and threat states.
- **Performance-avoidance goals** These are where the performer is striving not to be the worst performer within a competition or on a particular team. The emphasis here is negative as the athlete is trying to avoid failure.

Imagine Scenario 1 where you are asked to take a potential match-winning free in a hurling game. It is eighty yards from goal. The referee tells you it's the last shot of the game. If you score, the team wins their first county title. How would you approach the shot? How does your body feel? What thoughts are going through your mind? What are your chances of converting this free? What are the chances of not converting it? How important is success to you in this scenario?

Imagine Scenario 2 where you are asked to take a free to draw the game. Your team is losing by a point. It is eighty yards from goal. There is a breeze blowing against you. The rain is making conditions for striking tougher. The referee tells you it's the last shot of the game. If you score, the team gets a replay. If you miss, the team loses the county final and is out of the championship. How would you approach the shot? How does your body feel? What thoughts are going through your mind? What are your chances of converting this free? What are the chances of not converting it? How important is success to you in this scenario?

If you score in Scenario 1, you are the hero and can win the game for your team; if you miss, there is still a chance the team can win the replay. The potential gains are more noticeable than the potential losses.

If you score in Scenario 2, you have done your job, but there is still a chance the team could lose. If you miss, you are the villain as your team has been knocked out. The potential losses are more significant than the potential gains.

Typically, when you are faced with a difficult task where the potential losses are particularly relevant and might be used as motivation, then perceived pressure is inflated and performance for the most part decreases.

The task difficulty did not change. It is your perception of the event that causes pressure – the importance of it to you, the gravity, the consequences of failing. Take these factors away and most situations are easy for you.

Your reflections on how you would feel going into these situations are not based on the task (hitting a ball eighty yards) but usually on your expectations. How you evaluate this situation will have a big impact on how you respond.

Your mind tends to have a primary and secondary evaluation process. The primary evaluation is about how relevant the goal is to you and what the chances of success are. The secondary evaluation is based on the demands of the situation, such as expectations and pressure. You are faced with danger (physical and esteem), uncertainty and judging the effort required (mental and physical) to succeed.

You then look at the resources you have to meet these demands. Your evaluations of all these areas will influence whether you go into a challenge state or threat state. When you evaluate it as a challenge, then you connect into your physical and mental resources to meet that demand. When you appraise it as a threat, your physical and mental resources might feel inadequate and fail to meet the demand.

So, what does it feel like when you are in a threat state approaching situations where success matters?

Your primary thought might be that this goal is very important to you. You might not feel that success is possible, or you could feel that it is possible, but that you do not believe you have the resources to succeed. You are worried that you won't have the ability to meet the challenge (perceived low confidence) and worried about things outside your control, be it other people or conditions (low perceived control). Your focus might be on making mistakes and what could go wrong (avoidance goals). You may believe that people will think you're a failure. That you'll look stupid after all the training and sacrifices. That you are 'useless' (danger to self-esteem).

Your thoughts and perception start to create a negative mental approach. What occurs in the body at this point?

You have a less efficient cardiovascular response, marked by an unchanged or reduced amount of blood pumping from your heart per minute, and an increase in vascular constriction from normal resting levels. You start to feel an increase in your heart rate but, in this threatened state, your heart pumps inefficient blood to the brain and other areas of your body necessary for sports performance. The delivery of glucose and oxygen to your brain is inefficient. Your stress response is fight or flight, producing more cortisol (the stress hormone) than adrenaline.

You're unable to make clear, calm and correct decisions. You are unable to move as quickly and sharply and are not as co-ordinated as you normally are. You start to overthink learned skills. You start to do things outside of your skillset. You start to forget your positioning and role on the field. The most basic skills become rigid and difficult to do. You are overthinking every move. You are feeling overwhelmed. You want to escape this pressure. The harder you concentrate, the worse you seem to play. The harder you try, the more your control breaks down.

We have all experienced this threat state. It starts with your perception of a situation. The good news is that you have a lot of control, mostly over your own perceptions. You can change the demands, expectations and pressure you place on yourself. You can adapt how you perceive the demands being placed on you. Being in a threat state is not static. You can adapt and change your own resources to meet those demands. You can learn to be aware of your responses under pressure.

Become aware of how your body feels before and during pressure situations. How you interpret these feelings in the moment will help you to reach this 'challenge state' more consistently. Being aware of your thoughts leading into and during pressure situations is a critical skill too. Your thoughts and feelings affect your sports performance. How you understand and identify with them will be the difference between success and failure.

Mental training

Can you learn to perceive and face pressure positively and perform consistently in situations that matter to you? The answer is yes.

You might have been told at some point that 'pressure is bad'. That you or your family or your team don't handle pressure well. That you are mentally weak. These are all lazy assumptions and quick judgements. But where do they come from? Did your brain or another person discount all the things that you did well in previous games? Did you not show in those moments that you had the skills and resources to cope in perceived pressure situations?

Exercise

DEVELOPING SELF-BELIEF

In this exercise, I would like you to recall a successful game in which you played. Fill out your responses in the table on the next page.

A SUCCESSFUL PERFORMANCE RECALL	COMMENTS
How relevant was the game for you?	
What made conditions favourable for success in your view?	
What were you feeling before and during the game?	
What were you focused on before and during the game?	
What were you thinking before and during the game?	
What were you doing before and during the game?	
What strengths and skills did this performance show that you had?	

Now, I would like you to do the same for an unsuccessful performance.

You probably found that the only difference between them was your mental approach or perception. You did not lose your technical or movement skills, or your knowledge of how to play the game or how to execute your role on the pitch. Your negative mental approach (your perception of the challenge) impacted your ability to think clearly and to believe in yourself and your resources to cope with the demands in front of you.

It is possible to develop your own positive mental approach for getting into your challenge state. This will enable you to perform more consistently in pressure situations and to fulfil your potential.

When you are entering the performance zone, how do you know which challenge or threat state you are in going into it? There are four options.

1. **High challenge**

   You perceive that the goal is very important to you and that the conditions are favourable for you to succeed.

   You perceive that you have enough resources (self-belief in your ability, perception of control and process goals) to meet the challenge. You are focused on approach rather than avoidance goals; you feel a high perception of social support and believe you can perform to meet the challenge.

   You are more likely to feel positive – if you experience some negative feelings, you reframe them as positive, because your mind and body are producing efficient energy, attention and motor skills to help you perform.

2. **Low challenge**

   Low challenge occurs when the goal is very relevant for you and the conditions are favourable for you to succeed.

   The difference here is that you perceive that you do not have sufficient resources to meet the challenge. You are low in self-efficacy, have low perception of control over skills, focus on avoidance goals and have low perception of perceived support – consequently, you believe you cannot complete the challenge successfully. You deem the situation as being favourable to success, but your personal resources are not there to achieve it.

You are likely to experience positive and negative feelings, but you view negative feelings as unhelpful to performing. The mind and body respond less quickly to your needs and so produce less energy and, as a result, your attention is affected and your motor skills are weakened.

3. High threat

The challenge has high importance for you, and you want to succeed at it, but you do not feel conditions are favourable for you to succeed.

You feel you have insufficient resources to meet the demands. You believe you cannot overcome this threat or the unfavourable conditions. You experience negative emotions – low-level responses in your mind – that are seen as debilitative to performance, and you experience unhelpful approaches to performing, such as inefficient energy, distraction and poor motor skills.

4. Low threat

Your goal has high relevance for you, but you do not believe conditions are favourable for you to succeed.

You feel you have the resources to meet this challenge. With high levels of self-efficacy, high perception of control, a focus on approach goals and high social support, you feel you can overcome the threat.

You experience both positive and negative feelings, though you feel the negative feelings are facilitative. Your mind and body perceive less threat. Your cardiovascular response is better, and you have more energy, better attentional control and fine motor skills. You believe you can perform.

It is important to highlight at this point that challenge and threat states are not static: you can move from one to the other within a match as the brain's natural default is often negative and seeing the negative in situations. You can very quickly appraise the situation as a threat, but by changing what you focus on you realise you can meet the challenge, for example concentrate on something that is within your control rather than obsessing over what is not; be aware of how you speak to yourself; think about what skills you have to meet the challenge and focus on key tasks you can execute now.

As mentioned previously, your brain is hardwired to scan for threats and it has mental filters, so it doesn't get overloaded with information. You can quickly dump out relevant and irrelevant information from your subconscious. You can re-evaluate situations to alter your view of the demands and highlight your resources to meet them.

Achieving a challenge state

When faced with an important performance situation, how do you assess it? Below are the steps you can take to give yourself the best chance to get into your challenge state and perform at your best in pressure situations.

Step 1: primary evaluation

You have a knockout championship game coming up. How important to you is success in this game? High, medium or low? The most likely answer is high.

Now, given the preparation you have had throughout the year, what do you think your chances of success are? High, medium or low? Just a quick judgement is necessary for now.

QUESTIONS	COMMENTS
How important is this knockout championship game to you? High, medium or low?	
What do you think are your chances of success? High, medium or low?	

Step 2: secondary evaluation

This is where you look at the demands of the situation and how you perceive them. Is there danger present? What is the threat of getting hurt or injured (high, medium or low)? What is the danger to my esteem (we covered this in Chapter 2)? These perceptions can be based on your expectations: 'Can I handle this challenge and am I good enough?' It could be your perception of what others will think of you if you fail. It could be your perception of the consequences and what will happen if you fail (de-selection for the next game, criticism on social media, feelings you have let people down, anxieties over a contract not being extended, worries about finance).

The next area we focus on is uncertainty and what is in your control and what you must accept is not in your control. Do you feel in control of your skills? Do you have a high, medium or low perception of control?

Area three focuses on the requirement of effort, both mental and physical, to achieve success. Do you feel a high, medium or low effort will be required?

Step 3: resources to cope

This is where you assess the skills and resources you have at your disposal to cope with the challenge in front of you.

You are told by your manager that you will be marking one of the opposition's best forwards. How do you view this game now? Do you believe you can cope with the speed, strength and skills of your opponent? Do you feel fit and ready? What is in your control? What is your plan to deny your opponent possession? What is your plan when your opponent wins possession? What could you do with the ball that would make it difficult for your opponent to mark you? What can you do when your teammates have the ball that would make it difficult for the opposition?

With these questions, you might begin to realise that it won't be just about marking your opponent. You can have an impact on the game in many other ways. *You* decide before the game that when your teammates have the ball that you will be constantly moving to support them or give them an option to pass to you. Your opponent will have to use different skills and energy to mark you in these situations. This can influence how much energy your opponent has when they get the ball, and their decision-making might deteriorate the more tired they become.

What is your perception of this challenge? What skills and behaviours do your opponents display at their best or at their worst? What skills do you have that could help you meet some of these demands?

What might tip the contest in your favour are your high self-efficacy (belief in your ability to execute skills in a given task), high perceived control (that you have control over your skills), high focus on approach goals (clear focus on specific task-oriented actions that will help you perform) and that you have a perception of high social support from the people that matter to you.

Step 4: mind and body responses

When you approach challenging situations, you can often move between positive and negative feelings. When you interpret these feelings as helpful to your performance, you are likely to move towards a more challenging state. This supports your mind and body in producing enough glucose, oxygen and blood flow for efficient decision-making, co-ordination and attention control. When you interpret these feelings as unhelpful to your performance, you are likely to move towards a more threatening state.

Some perceptions and practices that are important to know and do

1. **It is not a situation that causes us to feel anger, anxiety or lack of confidence. It is our perception of that situation.**

   It all starts with your beliefs about yourself, and the person or the situation. You believe a person has mistreated you or blamed you. You feel anger towards them. How do you express that anger? Do you shout at them? Do you physically fight them? Do you speak to close friends about how their behaviour made you feel? What is the healthiest response?

You have an upcoming game that is important to you. What do you tell yourself? 'I need to succeed in big matches. I can't afford to fail. I can't let people down.' You place a rigid demand on yourself, and you start to have negative feelings about the match. You might tell yourself that 'failure is terrible', that 'I am such a failure – I am always losing'. These are unhelpful thinking patterns when we genuinely believe them to be true. Your perception of danger is amplified – the danger, in this case, is to your esteem. You are now threatened by the danger of embarrassing yourself and others or letting them or yourself down.

The good news is you can alter your perception of the situation. You can start to affirm a new belief about it. This new belief might be, 'I want to succeed. I love the challenge of these matches. I know it requires a lot of physical and mental effort to be successful. I am ready for this and trust my skills to perform. I know it won't all go to plan. I know I will make mistakes. It is not a perfect game.'

You might give yourself some additional perspective: 'The people who matter to me will still be my family, friends and teammates even if we win or lose; my career outside of sport will be there and I will still have a home to return to; there are over seven billion people who do not care how this game goes!'

You might address a new perspective on failure: 'I know when playing against teams and players of similar ability that failure is possible. It is tough losing, but I know I can learn from losing as much as from winning. It is part of sporting careers that teams win and lose at different stages. These are opportunities to learn and grow from.'

Checking what words you use around your perception of situations, yourself and other people takes awareness. How often do you use phrases like 'I need to'? Can you replace these with more helpful ones like 'I want to' or 'I can' or 'I will' or 'I have' or 'I am'? Or 'My performance was useless, awful' to 'My performance was disappointing, could have been better'. These words will help you to feel less shame, guilt and embarrassment around disappointments. What you say out loud, you say to your mind!

Recognise the unhelpful feeling and perception your thinking can create. Challenge the evidence of it. Replace the old statements with new empowering language. Practise it.

2. **Pressure is not bad, and goals being important does not cause pressure.**
Start to see pressure as a good thing, a privilege. You are doing something you care about and have been trusted with the responsibility of completing because you're capable and competent. Embrace the challenge and opportunity in front of you; it enables you to stretch and grow as a person.

Your mind and body are getting ready to perform. You are on the edge of doing something great. It is not the other person, situation or environment that causes your feelings and behaviours, it is your beliefs. When you become aware of them, you can start to change them to more affirming and empowering stories. You can learn to master them and create the story you want.

3. **Increasing your resources will help you to meet demands**

    Visualise the situation you want to be successful in. Focus on the person you want to be. Here is a sample script (about taking a free in hurling) that you can rehearse and practise.

    'I am calm, confident and in control. I take the ball from the referee; I remind myself I have practised these types of frees thousands of times and have scored from them many times (increase self-belief in the moment). I know my routine. I place the ball; I take three slow breaths through my nose and exhale until I feel all the air has left my body (change states to calm with a relaxed focus). I place my shoulders in line with the goal, I line the ball up with my left foot. I visualise the ball going over the black spot six feet over the crossbar. I rehearse my lift and feel the fluid strike in my mind (approach goal). I take one final breath. I pick the ball and commit fully to my strike. I see the ball flying over the bar. I love these moments.'

    Imagine a competitive situation as realistically as you can, with sights, sounds and feelings. Your brain starts to respond in similar ways as if you were facing that situation right now. So, you can learn to be composed, confident and in control in these moments. You can prime your mind and body to be the person and athlete you want to be.

4. Practise acceptance

In your performance environment, it is important to accept the things you can and cannot control. Being aware of these before and during competition and having a response plan is very important in terms of staying in control.

Focusing on the things you *can* control helps to reduce irrational and illogical thinking and gives you more self-belief in the moment. When you succeed at these small tasks, you get small doses of positive feelings, which encourage you to persist at tasks for longer.

What is controllable in your performance environment?	What is uncontrollable in your performance environment?
Effort, communication, attention, preparation, my responses and my behaviours, etc.	Other people's opinions, officials, weather, etc.

Look at the example in the table above and make a list of the things that are controllable and uncontrollable in your performance environment. List as many things as are relevant for you and that you tend to focus on. Remember: when you focus on aspects of performance you *cannot* control, you waste vital energy and mental resources. Notice when your attention is in the green and when it drifts into the red. How does your body feel and how do you tend to react when focused on things you can't control?

5. Taking control

- **Self-talk** Practising what you say to yourself will dictate your confidence, perception of control and approach at any moment. Practise statements before events, such as 'I am confident, committed and composed.' During adversity, 'I love to show my strength even when my performance is not going to plan. I can win the next ball.' Practise short cue words to increase focus, such as 'Find space and call for the ball', and energy, 'I am powerful'.
- **Preparation** Have a clear routine in the lead-up to events. It saves your energy for the most important decisions during the event (see Chapter 3).
- **Effort** Keeping your effort and energy levels high when practising and performing is a key cornerstone of success, learning and improving (see Chapter 8).
- **Communication** Observing and listening for key cues in training and games from team members will accelerate your performances. What is your body language like before and after certain plays? Take the time to reflect on your communication after training and what you tend to do well and where you can improve.
- **'What if' plans** Start to identify situations in training or games where you feel a lack of confidence or control or where you only want to avoid failure. Try to come up with a plan for them, for example 'When I concede a score in a game, I can go quiet and criticise myself. The next time this happens, I will communicate positively to my teammate where to run or what we can do next.'

On the pitch

Myself and Gerry Hussey had a huge and exciting challenge in 2016 when working with the Tipperary senior hurlers. Many of the squad had lost All-Irelands in 2009, 2011 and 2014, and had taken a hammering from Kilkenny in 2012. They had also lost narrowly in the All-Ireland semi-final in 2015. These defeats had left their mark on the team's confidence: they were struggling to believe they could win important matches, and there were a lot of negativities towards the team.

The demands on them had also changed from when they first started out. A lot of these players had won minor, Under-21 and senior All-Irelands very early in their careers, and there was an expectation that they should be winning senior All-Irelands regularly. Players like Paudie Maher, Brendan Maher, Noel McGrath, Bonner Maher and Séamie Callanan were seen as a golden generation, and when they failed to live up to supporters' high expectations, they were being discarded as 'mentally weak', 'bottlers' and not able to win tight games. Players and management were in a threatened state approaching important games. They were feeling a heavy sense of pressure. There was a lack of freedom and enjoyment in the group, and there was a lack of belief in their ability to succeed.

You could get a sense of the lack of confidence in the team when they were in tight games. You could also see the brilliance of these players behind closed doors in training – the skill levels, the fitness, the speed of thought and movement were a joy to behold. But if they were behind when a game approached the closing stages, there seemed to be a tension and tightness to them.

This unfolded again in their 2016 league quarter-final defeat to Clare. Players seemed to lack energy, made poor decisions and struggled to execute key skills. You could see the team in a threat state, not performing to their capabilities. It was time to get to work on helping them change their perception of themselves. If they believed they were bottlers, then it was highly likely they would hit the threat state repeat button when faced with important situations in the championship.

We wanted to create a vision that was more powerful than any negative memories from the past. We wanted to create a new self-belief about who they wanted to be, one that was positive and specific to them, and to create controllable behaviours that would make them proud.

This would move them from a threat to a challenge state. We spoke about why this team mattered to us. What success would mean to us. What we wanted our identity as a group to represent. We built our identity from a place of love, family, selflessness and ruthlessness. We focused on what was within our control – in our language, our preparation and our performances. We built high levels of support within our team. We gave positive feedback and reinforcement at every opportunity. We allowed ourselves to be open and receptive to feedback that would improve us and the team. We focused on the resources we had in our team and dressing room.

We believed that by getting the best out of everyone individually and collectively, we could be successful again. We looked at the season ahead and focused on our preparation, process and performance measures that were heavily focused on a mastery approach to our goals.

We took each game as a learning experience and reflected on what went well and where we could do better. We chose to listen less and less to outside noise. This helped to create and strengthen new beliefs for the team. We practised ways to build our resources daily.

Firstly, we developed high self-confidence by visualising successful moments, having images of the team at its best in the dressing room, replaying clips of past achievements and accomplishments, having verbal encouragement and positive self-talk.

Secondly, we developed a high perception of control through the practice of core skills in a competitive training environment. This enabled players to maintain a greater focus in stressful situations. We developed the physical, mental, tactical and technical skills needed to deal with the demands of intense games. We educated the players on lifestyle needs, positional needs and psychological needs for their roles.

Thirdly, we focused on mastery-approach goals that would enable consistent high performances. We aimed to improve our personal best and previous performance standards. We built profiles for each player, covering what was required for their position and what tasks they would perform. The players built great lifestyle habits that fuelled their approach to success too, in terms of goal-setting, sleep, nutrition, recovery and spending time with people and on activities that replenished them.

Fourthly, we focused on developing high levels of social support in the group, recognising the strengths and capabilities that each person added. Everyone was supportive, encouraging and looking out for one another.

This approach enabled players to experience more challenge states than threat states on a consistent basis.

These practices helped build a group of players who were clear about what success meant to them. With a shared vision, purpose and identity, they were excited about fresh opportunities rather than being burdened by the past or threats in the environment. They went on to achieve their outcome goals such as Munster and All-Ireland champions in 2016 by sticking to this process the whole way to Croke Park.

Summary

When facing situations that are important to you, your mind and body can react in different ways. To help you fulfil your potential, a challenge state is beneficial, whereas a threat state hinders your performance.

What can you do to ensure you enter this challenge state?

Firstly, you evaluate the goal as being relevant to your success as an athlete. You assess if success is possible.

Secondly, you evaluate some of the demands/expectations you place on yourself. Do you perceive physical danger to your health? Do you perceive mental and emotional danger to your esteem? Do you perceive uncertainty around this situation? What is controllable and uncontrollable about this situation? Do you set goals that approach success or avoid failure? What levels of social support do you have around you?

Just because you appraise the goal as important and success as possible, it does not mean you will automatically be in a 'challenge state'. You must ensure that your own resources, such as high self-confidence, high perceived control, focus on approach goals and high perception of social support, are in place. This will enable you to balance the scales from the demands being strong to the resources being even stronger.

When your resources are stronger than the demands, you are far more likely to perceive any negative feelings as energy towards your performance. This, in turn, enables your mind and body to produce the efficient energy, physical functioning and attention control to perform optimally.

Spending time on this mental preparation will ensure you approach important situations with greater belief in your ability, feeling more in control of your skills and feeling focused on the controllable behaviours needed to succeed. You will realise that uncomfortable moments and feelings will pass, and that you will be able to handle them. You will experience positive expectations towards your performances on a consistent basis.

5

PANIC VERSUS COMPOSURE

YOU CAN LEARN A LOT ABOUT HUMAN BEHAVIOUR from sport, in relation to composure, panic and being in control. In the final minutes of games, when the scores are close, who are the players who raise their performance levels and drive their team to success? Who are the ones who become passive and whose performance level drops? Who are the ones who maintain consistent performance levels? Who are the ones who try too hard and whose performance consequently deteriorates? Which players tend to freeze and make little contribution?

You can see subtle differences between those who succeed and those who don't. As fatigue of the mind and body start to kick in, you notice different traits appearing. Certain players grow in presence as the game enters the final moments. They stand taller, their head is up, they are on the balls of their feet. They are alert and lively. Their eyes are laser-like on their task at hand. They are fully present and connected to their teammates. They are relentless in competing for everything within their control. Their intensity is at just the right level – not too high in their mental or physical intensity where panic could kick in, and not too low where lethargy, distraction or flatness could take over. Their intent is to approach the challenge rather than avoiding mistakes or failing.

In the same circumstances, some players can shrink in presence as the fear of failure becomes dominant. You might observe a change in their energy levels. Their shoulders and head drop. They become flat and static on their feet, and indecisive in their movements. Their eyes begin to pick up too much information and, mentally, they struggle to focus on the target and to make decisions. They can become caught up in outcome-based thinking – past-based thinking around what happened or future-based thinking about what might happen. Their intensity might become too high, where they feel panicked or overwhelmed. Their behaviours become avoidant. They communicate less. They take fewer risks. They are predominantly on the back foot.

Other players again may step into fighter mode when their sympathetic nervous system is activated (see Chapter 2). They become overly aggressive or try too hard to fix everything on the field, and they forget their role and positioning. They may start to fight with officials, opposition players and teammates. Their focus on the target, first touch and decision-making are erratic. They lose their sense of control. They are failing to think clearly and execute the task at hand. They are feeling rushed in their movement and decision-making, and they use up energy very quickly in this panicked state.

They have failed to manage their mental approach. Their mind and body have been hijacked by negative thoughts, feelings and behaviours. They are in a state of panic and unable to access their skills and talents, and unable to access the rational, calm and creative side of their brain.

Recognising the negative mindset

When you have felt panic approaching important situations, was it hard to concentrate on the target or tasks in the present moment? Did your mind have racing thoughts and competing information? How did you feel emotionally – panicked, overwhelmed or anxious? How did you feel physically – tense in your chest, shaking, slightly nauseous? These are some of the mental, emotional and physical patterns you might notice when you are in panic mode.

Your fight response may kick in, prompting you to get rid of these feelings. Your freeze mode might kick in, where you become passive in your behaviours and withdraw your effort mentally or physically. You might go into flight mode and try to escape or avoid the situation.

When your heart rate is elevated, your body temperature changes and your breathing changes. You generally perceive these signs as a threat and are probably thinking, feeling and behaving like you can't cope. As we have learned, when your brain senses a strong threat, it kicks into fight, freeze or flight mode to protect you. You can feel a loss of control in some situations.

It is important to understand the different ways that our central nervous system responds to stress. Dr Stephen Porges' polyvagal theory is a study based around the feelings of safety. Essentially, when humans feel safe, their nervous systems support the homeostatic functions of health, growth and restoration, while they simultaneously become accessible to others without feeling or expressing threat or vulnerability.

The chart on the next page by Ruby Jo Walker will be helpful for you to identify what states you are accessing during the day, prior to and during your performances.

As you move through your day, your central nervous system will experience different states of expression. These multiple states can happen at lower levels of intensity, all at once or you can move through them like a ladder effect.

At the top of the ladder is social engagement (connection and safety), in the step below that is sympathetic activation or mobilisation (fight or flight – danger is present) and the bottom rung of the ladder is dorsal vagal shutdown (immobility – energy conservation). When in competitive environments, like playing a match, you most definitely move through these stages frequently as your brain assesses the different stimuli in your environment. You concede a goal: what state might your body move into? You score a goal: what state might your body move into? You win a big catch

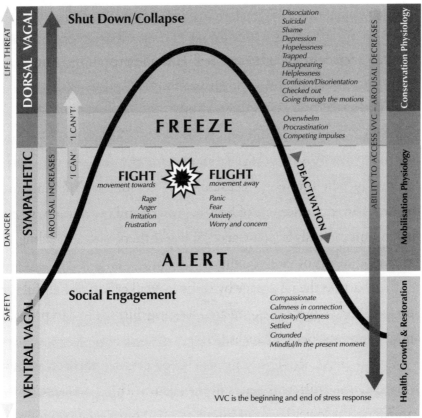

and are fouled, resulting in a roar from the crowd: what state might your body move into? You take a pause and breathe consciously through your nose and ground your feet: what mental state might you move into?

First is the social connection safety state, which is controlled by your parasympathetic nervous system. You feel a sense of safety, connection and groundedness. You can connect and relate to other people. You can empathise with them. You can read their facial expressions accurately. You are present and can access states of joy, playfulness and love. You feel safe, secure and happy. Groups in this state can co-regulate each other. You can feel calmness, openness and presence in your movements and awareness. Teams with high levels of trust in each other, their process and their plan live in this state more frequently than teams with lower levels of these things.

The second state is sympathetic activation, or mobilisation. This is your fight or flight response and is controlled by your sympathetic nervous system. You are in action or survival mode. In fight mode, you might move towards the threat, with feelings of anger, rage or frustration – high-energy feelings and hyperarousal. When in flight mode, you may feel anxiety, fear or panic and you start to move away from the threat. You may need to fight or flee to release the threat you are feeling. When performing we need to move from connection to action mode to get the task completed. What's important is how quickly we recover between these bursts of action. If we stay too long in fight or flight when we are performing, we can use up energy very quickly and this will impair our movement and decision-making, particularly in the closing stages of a match, which is when most games are won.

The third state is the freeze state, which is controlled by the parasympathetic nervous system. The freeze state is considered the most primitive, where you conserve energy, slow down and recover. It is impossible for your body to keep producing cortisol and adrenaline in your fight or flight state. Your body knows when to cap this production and return to a state of collapse or freeze. You can often feel lethargy, despondency and a lack of motivation.

Your brain has been built to protect you and scan for threats in your environment. In the modern world, your threats can be switched on all the time where traffic, deadlines and demands of life are very high. You can move between safety, fight, flight or freeze states throughout the day. This can affect your energy levels from a mental, emotional and physical perspective. It can affect your digestion, recovery and cognitive performance levels too. It can be difficult to connect with others, regulate your central nervous system and perform at your best when you are feeling threatened most of your waking hours.

It is important to be aware of what states you are in throughout the day. For you to be at your best for training and match day, you will need self-awareness to understand your predictable responses to stress – how your body responds in these states and how to activate or down-regulate your system. You will need to develop this self-awareness to identify which response you are in at any given moment and to use tools, such as self-talk, breathing routines, mindfulness, meditation and other reset triggers, to take you out of panic and back into composure and connection to yourself, your present moment and your task at hand.

My journey to composure

We were playing Tipperary in the 2010 All-Ireland hurling quarter-final in Croke Park. They had been tipped for the All-Ireland by many after narrowly losing the previous year's final to Kilkenny. Having lost several quarter-finals in Thurles down the years, it was a positive for us to be in a different environment for this challenge. Some of us had been involved in a great quarter-final win over Tipperary in 2005, which evoked good memories for us that we could do it again.

Most of us had had early success with Galway, winning Under-18 and Under-21 titles in Croke Park, which helped us to feel more grounded playing there. We had a three-week build-up to the game. I felt we had prepared well with a training camp in Johnstown House developing task cohesion around our roles and responsibilities on the field and social cohesion among the group. We had a very good team meeting, and we reiterated the belief we had in each other.

Our manager John McIntyre asked me to speak to the group about what it felt like to miss out playing for Galway in 2009 and what I saw in this team now. There was a strong emotional energy in the room, and as more and more players spoke about what the team meant to them, it brought us closer together. Players showed vulnerability to one another and there was a new connection forming in the team that I had not experienced previously.

Going up to Dublin on the bus on the morning of the quarter-final, I felt that we were very well prepared for the match. We had played several important games together that season – three in the Walsh Cup, a National League campaign that had culminated in winning the title and three Leinster championship matches. We were very match-fit and battle-hardened.

We all had good routines on game day and were well practised in terms of travel, food and warm-ups. We were well motivated to bring a huge performance.

I started the game extremely well. I was commanding my area on low and high balls. I was reading the play and making interceptions. I was supporting my teammates and linking the play from back to front. In the first twenty-five minutes, my direct marker had one possession, which he put wide. I felt I was in control of our contest.

Tipperary made a change and brought on Seamus Callanan at centre-forward. He was an incredibly skilful player and score-getter for them. I won the first couple of balls between us and felt composed and in control. Then, during the last few minutes of the first half, a high ball came down the middle. Our wing-back and full-back both hesitated and left the ball for each other to catch. I waited outside for the break or the pass. I lost sight of Séamie for a second or two. As I was watching this play unfold, Séamie took a gamble that the lads might miss it. The ball broke through, and he had a free run on goal and stuck it in the net.

I remember in that moment telling myself that I should have tracked the run. The old version of me, weak in confidence, would have berated myself internally for five or ten minutes over that mistake. From the work I had done all season on resetting after each play, I was able to quickly bring my attention to the present moment, let go of the past and focus on how I could help the team. I took a breath to compose myself as I ran out to my position. I stood tall, reset my body language and made eye contact with my goalie. I had shifted my mental state from possible freeze mode (panic) to composure and connection to self and my teammates.

In the next few moments, their full-forward Eoin Kelly came out forty yards to let me know what a great goal he thought it was! He was roaring at me and geeing up Séamie. He was right in front of my face. I stared ahead towards our forwards and made no eye contact with him. At that moment I knew I was in control of my response. I knew that panicking was not going to help my composure for the next play. I took three deep breaths through my nose and reminded myself that I was having a great first half and that one play wouldn't define my performance.

Once again, I reset my body language – shoulders back, head up, on the balls of my feet – and faced the next puckout. I used my reset trigger, *Vamos*, which is the Spanish for 'Let's go'. I had learned this from Rafa Nadal's autobiography, *Rafa: My Story*. I bet Rafa never thought his trigger word would be used in Croke Park! It helped me to get back into focus on the next task at hand.

Mental training

When you are heading into events, being in control and feeling composed are key skills to have in your mind and body. To feel in control, it is important to know what to focus on prior to and during the event, and so you need a pre-competition plan. If you do not have a plan, your mind will drift to its default mode of scanning for threats, being in negative states (panicking) and negative thinking.

Exercises

EXERCISE 1: EVENT PLAN

Below are some questions to help you develop or refine your focus and refocus plan.

1. How do you want to focus prior to your event? What are you looking forward to? What are you grateful for so far this season? What is in your control regarding your preparation and performance? What is not in your control? What can you influence? What helps you to remain relaxed, calm and in control?
2. What statements can you repeat to yourself that help you get into your best focus?
3. What movements help you to get into your best focus? What tasks help you to switch on your best game focus?
4. Why is it important for you to be in your best focus for matches?
5. What should you do if you can't get into your best focus on your first attempt?
6. What can you do to maintain your focus?
7. Looking at previous events, what took away your focus from the task at hand? What helped to regain it?

On the next page is a sample event focus plan starting out the morning of the event, with an afternoon throw-in start time of 4 p.m. It can be beneficial to build these plans for 24–48 hours from an event to ensure you turn up in your best mental and physical state to perform.

WHAT I DO	INTENSITY	WHY I DO IT	WHAT I DO IF IT'S NOT WORKING
Morning of event – meditation	2/10	To feel calm and present.	Do some box breathing and remind myself I am excited.
Meal prep and consumption	1/10	To fuel mind and body.	Try liquid form, like smoothies and shakes.
Before leaving – task goals, write down my three most important tasks and the person I want to be	2/10	To focus on positive and specific goals for the game. To ensure I am task-focused and in control.	Visualise myself doing these tasks well and my response when something goes wrong. Watch video of best clips.
Pre-warm up – activation, breathing and stretching	3/10	To feel loose and ready.	Remind myself it's only activation and its okay to feel nervous.
Team warms-up – lock in my best intensity and focus	5/10	To feel switched on and ready to start the game.	Engage with teammates, communicate and breathe, focus on task at hand.
Replicate game situations – small-sided games	6/10	To get into team play, communicate, co-operate and co-ordinate.	Reset – box breathing, body scan and positive self-talk.
Before throw-in – I am ready	7/10	To remind me I am prepared and can do this. To focus on being alert and lively on my toes. To communicate and focus on the ball.	Embody alertness for the next ball. There will be opportunities to influence. Stay present.

WHAT I DO	INTENSITY	WHY I DO IT	WHAT I DO IF IT'S NOT WORKING
In-game – practise being positive, present and on task	6/10	To be in a positive frame of mind, present in the moment and having a task focus to be consistent on each play.	Recognise when negative, past/future or outcome focused. Breathe and return to positive self-talk and attention on the present task.
Post-game – be present, reflect in diary	3/10	To recall what I did well and how. To recognise what areas can improve and how. To learn from the experience.	Speak with coaches and teammates to gain clarity and perspective on performance.

After each event, it is important to evaluate your plan. How did it go? What areas went best? What can you improve on and how?

It is common for athletes to experience difficult feelings coming to an event. At times, you may feel worried, tense and anxious. It is important to accept these as just feelings and not become hooked on them or caught up in negative thinking cycles. You can practise connecting to the present moment using the mindful breathing exercise below. This can be done prior to events to focus your spotlight of attention on the present moment.

EXERCISE 2: PRE-EVENT MINDFUL BREATHING

1. Get comfortable, either sitting upright in a chair or lying down. Close your eyes. Tune into your breath; notice the air entering and leaving your body. Breathe in and out through your nostrils five times.

2. It can be normal for your mind to drift and wander. When you notice this, just come back to your breath. You can use the breath as your anchor to the present moment.
3. Now, place one hand on your stomach and one hand on your heart. Notice the rise and fall of your body on the inhale and exhale for ten cycles of breath. Again, when you notice your mind wandering bring it back through your breath and observe the body as it rises and falls. This helps us to deactivate our fight or flight response and feel more grounded, safe and connected.
4. Repeat these two breathing exercises, using the nostrils or the chest and stomach as your points of focus, as often as you like. This helps you to be present, connected and calm.

EXERCISE 3: PRE-EVENT BODY SCAN

The next exercise is the body scan, which will give you an awareness of what you are feeling in your body and where. I will also introduce some progressive muscle relaxation to help you release and let go of tension from your body and mind. You can record these exercises on your phone and practise daily.

1. As before, get comfortable, either sitting upright or lying down. Close your eyes. Tune into your breath; notice the air entering and leaving the body. Breathe in and out through your nostrils five times. When you notice your mind drifting, come back to your breath.

2. Place one hand on your stomach and one hand on your heart. Notice the rise and fall of your body on the inhale and exhale for ten cycles of breath.
3. Now, take a deep breath in and squeeze your two fists for a count of five seconds. Exhale and release any tension from the tops of the fingers, palms and wrists.
4. Take a breath and squeeze your shoulders up towards your ears for a count of five seconds. Exhale, drop the shoulders and release any tension from them, and from your upper back and arms. Breathe into this area and allow the full expansion to occur.
5. Now breathe in and brace your core muscles and chest for five seconds. Breathe out and release any tension in the stomach and chest area for a few breaths.
6. Now move your attention to your quads and glutes. Take a breath in and squeeze these muscle groups tightly for five seconds. Breathe out, expand and release the tension from these muscles.
7. Now bring your attention to your feet. Curl your toes up towards the head, breathe in for a count of five seconds and tighten all the lower body at once. Exhale and release any last tension from the lower body.
8. Gently breathe into your whole body from head to toe and gently scan for any areas that might feel tense.
9. Repeat the progressive muscle relaxation technique a few more times and see if you can release this tension further.

10. Gently open your eyes and notice how you feel in your mind and body.

It is very beneficial to have a best-focus plan heading into each event. This helps your mind and body focus attention on the steps in front of you and reduce the level of worry or concern. It also helps you to adjust if the plan is not maintaining your best focus or when you need to regain it.

Mindful breathing and body scan exercises enable you to detach from your thoughts. They will help you feel more in control, present and composed.

EXERCISE 4: IN-GAME BOX BREATHING

In times of stress, your sympathetic nervous system or stress response system is on high alert. Using techniques like box breathing, you can regulate this system to a calmer and more composed state, called the parasympathetic nervous system, which is known as the relaxation response system. This is the opposite of your fight or flight response.

When you are anxious or in a panicked state, your breathing becomes shallower. This can create more anxiety, panic and tension in your body. You can use your breathing to move from the sympathetic (stress response) to parasympathetic (relaxation response) in a matter of moments.

In my work with athletes, the use of breathwork has been one of the most effective exercises for grounding. The navy seals have developed a very useful technique called box breathing.

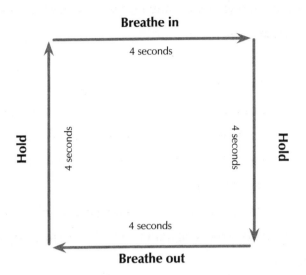

You begin with a breath in through the nose for four seconds, you hold at the top of the breath for four seconds, you breathe out for four seconds and you hold at the bottom of the breath for four seconds. Repeat this sequence four or five times and you will start to feel your mind becoming a little clearer, more rational, calm and logical. You will feel your body relax and release any tension from your shoulders and chest. You will begin to approach the next situation in a more composed state.

The breath has a powerful ability to send signals from your brain down through the vagus nerve into the central nervous system to activate your calm response. This can be done in a matter of moments with just a few breaths. This technique brings better focus, decision-making and movement.

On the pitch

With the Tipperary senior hurling team, we got the players to understand their stress responses and states. Over previous seasons, they had panicked in key moments in games, when fight, flight or freeze mode became dominant. They did not have the skills in those periods to regulate their systems to play with freedom, joy and love. We worked extremely hard throughout the season to build connection, composure and safety within the team. We allowed people to express how they were feeling going into games, what were their deepest fears and concerns. We worked on changing those fears to new beliefs about themselves and their teammates, and embracing the journey of learning, growth and mastery.

We worked on having very strong social support within the group, and we highlighted consistently what each team member was good at, what others were doing well and how the group was improving individually and collectively. We ensured we were a team that knew what we stood for. We focused on what we could control in relation to our expectations regarding our mindset, preparation and performances.

Week by week you could see the confidence and belief rising in the group. Players were beginning to express their authentic selves more and more on and off the field. You could sense that players and management were becoming more connected. That there was real enjoyment, fun and freedom in training and in the performances on match day. There was great energy, honesty and creativity in the performances that year, culminating in winning the 2016 All-Ireland title by beating champions Kilkenny, 2–29 to 2–20.

There were so many special moments during that campaign where the connection of the group and their support for each other stood out. One moment that showed lessons had been learned from previous experiences was in the semi-final win over Galway.

Halfway through the first half, our captain Brendan Maher had possession. He instinctively went to pass a ball inside to his teammate. The Galway forward Joe Cooney read the pass brilliantly and soloed through to score a goal. In previous seasons, this could have knocked the players into fight, flight or freeze mode. I observed Brendan in the next seconds. He took some deep breaths, he stuck his chest out, he lifted his head higher and started moving in a composed manner to his position.

Before the next puckout, he wiped his hurley under his arm to mentally wipe that play from his mind. He was back in the present and focused on the next play.

I started to see players connect with each other in those moments. They also knew how to down-regulate their fight or flight mode when things did not go to plan all the time. From the next play, they won possession and created and executed a score.

They knew they were in control of their response. They chose connection, composure and freedom. They did not allow their past experiences to disrupt them from doing what they wanted to do in the present. They knew they had the freedom and ability to choose their response.

Below are some practices that coaches can incorporate with their teams to develop composure and connection.

1. Share your dominant response to stress with the group when pressure comes on, for example fight, flight or freeze. Normalising it as a leader will enable others to share their typical responses.
2. Use language to normalise it – 'This is my red-head response (disconnected/distracted) when I become disconnected from the present, panicked or off-task. I use the anchor of my breath to reconnect to myself to the present moment and what can be referred to as my blue head (connected/concentrated) where I am connected, present, clear and calm.' Moving from red to blue head is a practice we can all get better at. We can use simple routines like feeling our feet on the ground or wiping our hands on our chest to come back into our bodies and into the present moment.
3. Discuss as a group the plan to help one another move to better mental states of composure, concentration and connection. What support do we need from each other in those moments? What techniques help us to feel grounded and connected? What helps us to focus on the task at hand? What type of language must we use?
4. Practise being in stressful situations together and reverting to the plan in the steps outlined above. Discuss what worked well and where we might need to refine it.

Summary

As you move through your day, your mind and body are constantly assessing and perceiving the world around you. Which situations are tipping you into overload and a panicked state and what are you focused on here? In what situations are you in composed and connected states and what are you focused on here? When your mind senses a threat, it naturally fires its response system, and you can enter a state of panic. But if you practise seeing the opportunity for growth in all situations, you can start to regulate your response system into a state of composure and connection.

In this chapter, we have spoken about the three main responses to stress:

1. Fight mode where you move towards the threat.
2. Flight mode where you move away from the threat.
3. Freeze mode where you shut down mentally and physically.

To be a top performer, you need to identify which situations trigger your different stress responses, and then reframe those moments as opportunities for growth. Become aware of how you behave when in freeze, fight or flight mode. When you recognise your behaviours, you can change them by using techniques such as breathwork to activate your calm response, at which point you start to feel safe, connected, present and can approach situations with composure. You can make better choices when not panicked or overwhelmed.

It is also important to identify before events what your best focus is – What is in your control? What is not in your control? What can you influence in your performance? How and when do you lose focus? Having routines for your brain to engage in that are action-related and within your control can help before and during key events. You can then adapt much more quickly when you observe negative patterns developing and reorientate back to your best focus.

6

DOUBT VERSUS CONFIDENCE

WINNING THE BATTLE WITH OURSELVES IS VERY often the difference between success and failure. This battle often involves our inner negative dialogue or voice, telling us what we can't do.

One of the keys to move closer to realising more of our potential is to focus our perspective on what we can do. What gives me the greatest confidence in myself is when I focus on the good things in my life, be it my positive traits, the positive people in my life or the positive experiences I have had.

When our inner voice is focused on the things we can't do,

haven't done, how life is unfair, tough and how other people do not support us, then it is highly likely we will experience self-doubt and not approach challenges in a positive way – or, worse still, not even take on challenges.

Our inner voice can give us many reasons why we should or should not do something. If we become over-attached to our negative thoughts, we can feel self-doubt in important moments. An important point is that we have little to no control over the thoughts that enter our minds; most are generated automatically. If we are waiting for the right thought to come or the right feeling to come before we do anything, it's unlikely we will achieve much in life. Instead, we need to just accept that they are constantly moving through us; this gives us more mental space and freedom to do what we need to do in any given moment. I can still make a run in a game regardless of what I am thinking or feeling. I can still communicate with my teammates or get on the next ball regardless of what I am thinking or feeling.

For me, different situations or events can trigger different thoughts and feelings of either confidence or self-doubt. My younger self often got caught up in a constant feedback loop of negative dialogue. Have I prepared well enough? Am I good enough to play at this level? What if my opponent runs at me – will I have the speed to cope? What if I am not fit enough to last the intensity of this game? I lost games before the ball was even thrown in because of this.

It is very normal to doubt ourselves, to feel fear, self-doubt and anxiety. We have already learned about our fight, flight or freeze system that kicks in when we feel under physical, mental or emotional threats. When facing a situation that will challenge us or take us outside of our comfort zone, we perceive mental and emotional threats to our sense of self with questions such as 'Am I good enough?', 'What will others think of me if I fail?', 'What are the consequences of failing?'

I might freeze in certain scenarios when I need to act. I might fight the situation I am in and become aggressive or resistant towards it. I might try and escape from it by fleeing the situation.

Physically, I get sweaty palms, my breath becomes shallow, my heart rate is pumping, I feel nauseous or my body shakes. I believe that I can't cope. I find it hard to concentrate and my mind is racing.

While these bodily changes can be good in times of crisis, helping us to recognise and cope with threat, knowing how to calm your nervous system is one of the greatest lessons you can learn – how to cope with uncomfortable responses, such as increased heart rate, sweaty palms and shallow breathing.

You can learn new ways to change your perception of situations, to assess these situations as a challenge rather than a threat (covered in Chapter 4). You can learn to place healthier and more positive expectations on yourself (see Chapter 3). You can learn what key resources you have within yourself that will enable you to adopt a challenge mindset of excitement and confidence rather than one of fear and self-doubt (see Chapter 4).

In this chapter, I will show you how you can move from self-doubt to confidence in any aspect of your life.

My journey to confidence

In the first part of my Galway career, from nineteen to twenty-five years of age (2003–2008), I felt a huge fluctuation in my confidence, from game to game and from season to season. If I performed well in a game, I trained well and enjoyed the week after the game. If I performed poorly, I found it very hard to recover and perform well in training or games for the next week or two.

I was very harsh on myself after mistakes or poor performances, feeling that I had let myself, teammates, management and family down. I was annoyed and frustrated, and I often isolated myself.

At times, it felt that no matter how hard I worked in the gym, in the alleys or on the pitch, I was not making progress, and I wasn't going to perform in the next match no matter what I tried. This self-doubt followed me around, as though my brain was hypervigilant to threat, mistakes and failures. I felt low in energy at training – if I missed a ball or did not start well, it would further compound the misery. I was constantly berating myself for my lack of ability when things went wrong.

When I got back on the senior panel after being dropped in 2008–2009, I decided I needed to refocus the mental side of my game. It was an aspect of my preparation that I had really let slip, so I was doubting my ability continuously and focusing on anything I had not done well or couldn't do.

Practising key mental skills like visualisation, hypnosis, positive self-talk and goal-setting when I worked with John McGuire in 2006 had been hugely beneficial, helping me to focus better on my strengths and what I could do and what I had done well in the past.

The visualisation helped me to have a more positive expectation of myself. I used positive affirmation scripts too and they helped me to change the image I had of myself as mentally weak under pressure.

I slowly began to reprogramme some of my self-limiting beliefs, which I spoke about in Chapter 1. I began to feel more confident in my abilities. I spoke to myself in a more positive way when I made mistakes. I became like my own best friend, supporting, helping and encouraging myself through obstacles. I felt less anxious before and during games. I was able to be more present in my performance through meditation and breathwork.

By getting back into this mental work bit by bit, I began to focus more on what I could do rather than what I couldn't. I began to see my strengths more clearly, shining through from each experience. I saw that I was one of the fittest and strongest people on the team, that I was a dominant, supportive and composed presence on the team. I began to use these qualities to my advantage. I began to use my focusing skills to anticipate situations faster than my opponent and used my vision and passing skills to a higher level because I was free from drowning in my own negative thoughts and feelings. I began to see teammates' movements faster. I began to get to the ball faster than my opponents through reading body-language cues. I felt incredibly alert and energised in my mind and body.

By quieting this negative inner voice of self-doubt through the work off the field, there was less noise and distraction going on in my mind. I was more engaged, connected and present to the task at hand more often. I was so locked into one moment at a time that everything before or after it just faded into the background. This new sense of confidence was so liberating. Because I was no longer drowning in my own self-doubts and limitations, I felt I could do anything and achieve anything on the field.

I had found a lovely flow to my process. I was doing the right things with the right amount of effort, intensity and quality. I was feeling fresh and ready for training and games. I had full confidence in my physical and mental preparation. I knew I was ready to compete and help the team in the important matches.

After each session and game, I highlighted in my journal what I had done well. I became very good at spotting the good and reaffirming to my subconscious mind through positive reinforcement, affirmations and journalling. The visualisation of up-and-coming events enabled me to focus better on what I could control, and I felt a sense of calmness and readiness approaching these important situations.

Recognising negative mindsets

Doubt – thinking about what might go wrong – is a natural feeling when you approach something that matters to you and that has consequence. Your brain senses threats and seeks to protect you from potentially harmful situations.

The threat, in this case, might be failing at something. You begin to feel nervous, tense, and you find it hard to focus on other aspects of your day or life. Most of your waking hours are consumed by negative thoughts and feelings around this event that is coming. This worry is using up vital energy resources that you need so you can be at your best come match day.

The worry or anxiety comes from fear – fear of messing up, fear of not meeting expectations, fear of letting others down, fear of failing, etc. Your mind tries to find ways to overcome these fears through thinking – but the more you get caught up in these thinking modes, the more power/energy your fear gets from it.

We must acknowledge at this point that it is not what happens – losing a match, not playing well – that causes self-doubt, fear and anxiety; it is our thinking that causes it. If we stop or reframe the thought, the feeling naturally dissipates. If we choose not to get attached to any thought, it will pass. This is why mindfulness, meditation and focusing on a behaviour can be so powerful. We can become aware of thoughts and sensations, but we do not become attached to them or consumed by them. We realise that we have the power to direct our perception and attention. We can practise moving from a judgemental mind, where we label things as good or bad, right or wrong, etc., to an open and aware mind that notices this critical mind but doesn't become attached to the thought itself.

When I first studied sport psychology I had three main realisations:

- How I think can influence how I feel and behave.
- How I feel can influence how I think and behave.
- How I behave can influence how I feel and think.

It's all intertwined.

Mental training

Our thoughts and feelings are like an electrical current running through us. The first lesson to remember is that when we encourage ourselves with positive and helpful words, we start to feel more empowered. With awareness, we can have more control of the present moment than we think. I can start to create and become aware of what the most confident version of myself tells me in important moments. This positive self-talk can help with my perspective, judgements, feelings and actions.

The second lesson I know to be true is that thoughts can happen automatically without our consent or control – but that self-talk *is* something we can control. Before important events, I ask myself what the most confident version of me (my inner warrior) wants to think, feel and behave like. You can do this too. You can review moments from your past when you felt at your most confident. You can reflect on what you were thinking and saying to yourself, what you were doing and how you were feeling. You can start looking at previous experiences that went well and learn some of the controllable factors/behaviours that you can repeat again.

You don't always have to feel and think and behave the same way in situations. You don't need to label yourself as a confident or unconfident person just because a situation you were in before did or didn't go well. You are not defined by your previous achievements, your memories of the past or the limited stories you tell yourself. Each day is a new day to define what confidence is for you, what success is for you, what happiness is for you, and you can choose to put your energy and attention into that.

You can choose to think in a different way by repeating positive, inspiring and helpful words to yourself and others. You can activate positive thoughts and feelings by choosing what you focus your energy and attention on, for example being grateful and thankful for the skills, qualities, people and resources you do have. You can behave in ways that align with who you want to be and the dreams you want to pursue. You can choose to surround yourself with people who positively encourage and support you to be your best. You can choose to release yourself from the people or stories that no longer nourish you with positive feedback or ambitions.

Develop your confidence

Confidence is something that can be developed and influenced by you and the environments you choose to be in. It is a state of mind that you experience, based on what you feel is achievable. You can create your own scorecard on what success is to you, so you can decide that state of mind for yourself.

For sport, confidence is a mental state empowered by the beliefs that a player has about executing specific skills to a desired level or achieving specific outcomes for themselves or the team.

My state of mind can fluctuate up or down from moment to moment, session to session or game to game. Factors that can influence my confidence can be recent performances, personal preparation, goals set for the team, personal goals, the perception of the situation, the demands placed on me by the opposition, coaches, social media, etc., how the team is doing, the ability of other players, the commitment of other players (or lack of), how much time is left in the game. The challenge as I see it is to develop a robust confidence that does not fluctuate massively up or down.

A very good framework for building self-confidence is Albert Bandura's model. Bandura is a cognitive psychologist best known for social learning theory, the concept of self-efficacy. He has defined self-efficacy as your belief in your ability to succeed in specific situations or to accomplish a task. Your sense of self-efficacy can play a major role in how you approach goals, tasks and challenges. The confidence you feel during a particular activity or in a particular situation is generally derived from one or more of the following six sources, listed in descending order of importance:

1. Performance accomplishments
2. Vicarious experience
3. Verbal persuasion
4. Physiological states
5. Emotional states
6. Imagery experiences.

Performance accomplishments is by far the most important source of confidence; most athletes or coaches when speaking about previous training or performances will reference what has gone well, how they have been successful before and how they can be again. They might reference the collective strengths and qualities of the team. Writing down or speaking about recent achievements or improvements feeds our confidence muscle.

The next most important source is *vicarious experience*. This means that when you watch other people perform successfully, it can bolster your own confidence. Watching someone else at a similar level, size or background perform a skill successfully can reaffirm a sense of belief that I can do that too.

Verbal persuasion or encouragement can help change attitudes and behaviours, including self-confidence, for example having someone credible and important to you remind you of your strengths and qualities, or saying positive and helpful things to yourself with emotion, repetition and conviction, such as: 'I am excited to perform today, and I know I have the skills and attitude to succeed.'

The fourth source of self-confidence is *physiological states*. It looks at how we cope with physiological responses to stress, such as muscular tension, changes in breathing or butterflies in the stomach. How we view these bodily sensations will impact our performance. Do you view them as facilitative or debilitative? Knowing the power of body language and breathing to activate inner calm and confidence is hugely important.

The fifth source is *emotional states*. Self-confidence is the emotional response of the body to various situations. If you are anxious approaching an event, it most likely will impact your confidence. Managing your thoughts and emotions leading up to and during events and employing positive self-talk will help maintain your confidence. What you put your attention on will affect what you think and feel. Learning how to tune out negative self-talk will enable you to relax and have enhanced attention skills, while knowing how to regulate emotional states in the moment will also impact your confidence and ability to perform the tasks at hand.

The sixth source is *imagery experiences* – using the power of your imagination and all your senses to achieve successful performances in your mind and body. The power of your subconscious mind to encode the key skills, feelings and actions required to be successful helps improve your self-confidence in learning new skills and adapting to new challenges.

Challenging your thoughts

I believe that it is vital to repeat daily when negative thinking occurs 'I am not my thoughts. My thoughts are not always facts, they are not always true.' It is extremely important to cultivate a self-awareness around what you say about yourself. What do you say about other people? What do you say about the world? What do you say about new or old challenges you encounter? How do you view failure? How do you view feedback? Are your words, feelings and behaviours increasing your confidence or lowering your confidence? Are you using empowering words or disempowering words?

If you have a poor view of yourself and your capabilities, then every negative and unhelpful statement you tell yourself will start to weaken your confidence in your abilities over time. If your teeth were getting dirtier day by day, you wouldn't not clean them. You believe oral hygiene is important to you and your health, so you brush your teeth daily. You must take the same approach to your 'thought/word hygiene' and challenge what you say to yourself when it is negative and unhelpful.

Unpack your faulty judgements, expectations and assumptions. Grab your notebook and write down the negative self-talk you're engaging in. What is stopping or holding you back from being successful this season? For example:

I am too young to succeed at this.

Is this fully true, somewhat true or not true at all?

'Not true at all, there are countless players my age who have played well and been successful at this level before.'

What is the evidence to support this statement, if any?

'There are young players and older players who have not succeeded but there are as many who have.'

What other evidence is there that it is false, that you were able to complete the task or had the skills necessary to be successful?

'I have played many good games in training against experienced players, and I have done it in several matches too.'

What does this tell you about what you are capable of?

'I have the athleticism, skill and determination to overcome this challenge now.'

What uncomfortable truth must you work on, and how?

> 'I need to ensure my focus is always on the task at hand. There will be times when things don't go well. I will work hard at not judging myself and my performance while always focusing on the next task.'

What is the new positive and empowering statement you can tell yourself now when approaching new challenges?

> 'I have the talent, a positive *can-do* attitude. I will have the work done and I have the skills necessary to be successful.'

This daily practice of 'word hygiene' in your notebook will produce a confidence you never realised you had. It will help you to view challenges as things to embrace rather than be fearful of. It will enable you to face new situations with a greater awareness of the faulty words and assumptions that were holding you back.

With this new awareness, you will be able to reframe your story to one of empowerment, one that will lift your motivation, elevate your attention to focus on the task at hand, and give you the ability to process key relevant information and let go of irrelevant distractions.

I will now share with you some of the mental training practices you can work on daily to create new pathways of belief in your mind and body.

Exercises

EXERCISE 1: AFFIRMATION – SCRIPTS FOR SUCCESS

I am an All-Ireland winner. I commit every single day to nourishing my body and mind with healthy food and water. I nourish myself with new and encouraging words, behaviours and experiences. I give my body the rest it requires every day. I bring a sharp focus to every session I do. I know each time I train and by how I act that I am growing into the great player I want to be. I build good habits daily through meditation, visualisation, goal-setting, breathwork and self-talk to enable me to have complete present-moment focus, calmness and confidence when completing the tasks at hand.

I know I am the fittest, strongest and fastest I have ever been. I know my striking, touch and awareness on the field is the best it's ever been. I love learning the game and getting better at everything I do. I love taking on new opponents and challenges. This enables me to grow my character and find out even more about who I am and what inner strengths I have. I realise there are tough and uncomfortable moments to overcome to pursue my dreams. I know that on the other side of tough things there are very rich memories and rewards.

EMPOWERING SELF-TALK	DISEMPOWERING SELF-TALK
I am ready to perform no matter what the task/challenge that comes.	I doubt I can perform the tasks that I am expected to handle.
I have the work done and trust my game.	I don't feel I have enough done and worry my game is not ready for this level.
I accept mistakes will happen, but these do not mean that I lack the ability to play my game to a high level.	I can't afford any mistakes today or I will fail and let others down.
Expected and unexpected things will happen today. I embrace the unexpected and trust my ability to focus on the task at hand.	I hate not knowing what might happen and I worry I won't be able to cope with the challenges.
I focus on what I can control: my attitude, effort and behaviour.	I hope I perform well so I won't let anyone down.
I can perform well today. I have the work done. I am ready to give it my best. With great focus, positive communication and huge effort I will help the team.	I *have* to perform well today. I can't afford to make any mistakes. I can't let my teammates and coaches down. There is no margin for error.

EXERCISE 2: ACHIEVEMENTS – VISION BOARD FOR SUCCESS

Identify some of your proudest achievements and accomplishments from your past and create a photo montage. Gather feedback from former teammates, opponents, managers and coaches. Identify some of the keywords and themes that resonate with you and include these on your vision board.

Include images of future goals you wish to achieve, for example playing on a particular team, in a particular stadium, winning an individual or team award. Think of the role models who inspire you. Add their image to your board and any quotation from them that resonates with you.

EXERCISE 3: HIGHLIGHTS – VIDEO CLIPS TO POWER THE MIND WITH CONFIDENCE

Create a short, inspiring video of your best plays from your previous games. Put together your key attributes on and off the ball. Include keyword values that you stand for (from Chapter 1) and that inspire you, such as 'relentless', 'composed' and 'ruthless'. Include any powerful images of past victories from your vision board, images or plays from your role model at his or her best and your key ambitions for the future. Put some inspiring music in the background that raises your energy and confidence.

Watch these plays on your phone and rehearse doing them in an upcoming game through visualisation. These will boost your confidence in the moment and before future challenges.

EXERCISE 4: BEST MENTAL STATES – IDENTIFY YOUR BEST DAYS

When you think back to your best performances, what three words would you use to describe yourself? What are you saying to yourself? What are you doing? What are you feeling?

These words might be 'relentless', 'focused', 'composed'. Break down the behaviours that feed these words.

1. **Relentless** I am always on my toes, looking for the ball and moving to support my teammates.

2. **Focused** I am fully in the present; I move out of the past quickly and I am communicating the next task to myself and others. I am energetic and committed to winning the next play.

3. **Composed** I am calm in my mind and body. I am doing things quickly, but I'm not rushed. I see my teammates and the opportunities on the field.

Think of specific moments when you were at your best recently. How were you thinking, feeling and behaving? What were you saying to yourself or your teammates? Now, before a game if you need a confidence boost, you can repeat to yourself your three keywords. They are aligned to the behaviours that are specific to you; they are positive and controllable: 'I am relentless, focused and composed.'

On the pitch

I love working with people who are motivated to write new stories and achieve great things for themselves, their family and the people they represent. Every athlete and team have doubters and there will be times when it is hard to ignore or not be affected by negativity from the outside. Such negativity can create self-doubt, which in turn can hamper your chances of realising your potential.

A team I worked with in recent years had set themselves the vision of becoming All-Ireland champions. It was something no team in their county had ever done before at senior level. There were no past accomplishments or vicarious experiences to relate to that could boost the players' confidence. So, in our first session together, we decided to use another source of confidence: 'our imaginal experiences'.

The subconscious mind is a wonderful resource when you know how to use it to your advantage. We all have a conscious mind and a subconscious mind. The conscious mind is very rational and logical. If the conscious mind is full of fear of what can and might go wrong, then the subconscious mind is reactive to these fear-based responses. If the conscious mind is full of love, peace, harmony, happiness, freedom and joy, then the subconscious will produce love-based responses. It is the captain of the ship, acting on orders that the conscious mind sends its way. If the conscious mind says, 'I can win an All-Ireland' or 'I am going to be an All-Ireland winner' or 'I am an All-Ireland winner', then the subconscious mind will engage with this perspective.

The thoughts I plant in my subconscious garden are the ones I begin to reap in my conscious mind (body and our external environment). I sow seeds of success and think quietly and with conviction of the qualities necessary to succeed.

With the right action in my body and environment, I start to see it come into existence. The subconscious does not know the difference between real and imagined experiences. When it accepts an idea, it begins working on executing it. When I accept it as truth, I will be successful in my chosen area. It will bring the best conditions, people and environment to enable it to happen.

Our thoughts, feelings and visualised imagery are the organisers of our current and future experiences. I become clear on the cause (for example to become All-Ireland champions with love, passion, enjoyment and freedom). I identify the thoughts, feelings and imagery that are associated with that cause. I start to experience it as if it has already happened through visualisation and meditation. I commit to right practices and actions daily that will affect our success, love, enjoyment and freedom.

With that team, we practised daily empowering statements of belief ('I am', 'I can', 'I have' and 'I will'). We practised meditation and visualisation. We became the captains of our own ships, the masters of our minds. We empowered ourselves with suggestions of belief, love, passion, joy, freedom and success.

Wonderful things began to happen and in less than twelve months we were All-Ireland champions.

How can coaches help their athletes to feel more confident in themselves?

Coaches can help their athletes to develop a confidence profile by asking them to:

1. rate the five most important traits that they believe confident athletes possess
2. rate their confidence in these self-selected traits
3. rate the causes of their confidence
4. plot this information into a confidence profile.

CONFIDENCE PROFILE		
Rank	Traits to be confident about	Meaning
1	Speed	Feeling fast, that I can be the first to the ball or beat an opponent.
2	Stamina	Feeling fit, that I will bring consistent energy throughout a game.
3	Strength	Feeling strong, that I can dominate 50/50 situations.
4	Sharpness	Feeling eye/touch is in when I receive the ball, can nail touch quickly to give me time to decide.
5	Being clear on role	Know my job and what's expected of me.
6	Getting in a good block of training	Putting multiple good sessions in over time together so that we feel prepared.
7	Feeling positive mentally	Feel ready to meet the challenge.
8	Being creative	Taking calculated risks on the ball.
9	Believing in teamwork	Players will help and cover for each other.
10	Trusting coaches	Feeling that coaches will support me through thick and thin.
11	Analysing opposition	Having knowledge of opposition strengths and weaknesses and how we can exploit them.

The athlete or coach can then ensure as part of their preparation that they feed these sources of confidence regularly.

There are five key coaching behaviours to improve athletes' confidence, according to Forlenza *et al.* (2018):

1. **Nurture a positive environment** Athletes believed that the coaches who promoted fun experiences and positively reinforced behaviours led to increased confidence. Facilitating successful experiences is important for confidence too, so matching athletes up against individuals or teams with mixed abilities can help provide successful experiences for many.
2. **Respond to athletes** Recognise good performances through praising effort and skills observed in them. Additionally, bring constructive criticism to areas the players can improve on and reinforce their strengths. Show the individual and the team how they have improved.
3. **Develop effective practices** Set and maintain high standards for athletes in training, hold them to accountability for their timeliness, effort, communication and goals for each session.
4. **Hone interpersonal skills** Coaches should tell their athletes how confident they are in them and remind them how well prepared they are and how hard they have worked. Spread this feedback to all panel members for unity and equality.
5. **Highlight interpersonal qualities** Provide information to athletes about what they need to do fitness-, strength- or performance-wise to meet the challenges ahead. Tell them why and how it will benefit their game and performances. Athletes

want to understand why coaches use certain practices and strategies. They also want coaches to help them control their emotions, such as anger and frustration.

Summary

Becoming aware of your natural responses to situations helps you to manage your fear and gain self-confidence. You can do this by practising what you say to yourself leading into and during an event. You assess the judgements, expectations and assumptions you are making about yourself and the situation. You challenge any faulty truths that are not empowering you and you write a new, empowering story that brings excitement and confidence. You do this by repeating powerful and affirmative words that will lead to new behaviours in the moment. Self-talk is something you can do. Thoughts, both positive and negative, naturally come and go.

There are many tools and practices that can help you move from fear to greater self-confidence. Reflecting on past accomplishments and what you did well. Looking at successful, inspiring role models and imagining yourself doing the same things and achieving success. Positive feedback from credible people. Being aware of how you think, feel and behave in situations in which you want to be successful and reframing what you say if it doesn't support your focus and motivation. Behaving in ways that empower your energy through breathwork and powerful body language.

You can and will do this. You are a strong, confident and resilient person. You have the skills, qualities and mindset to achieve great things in your life.

7

PESSIMISM VERSUS OPTIMISM

WHEN YOU ENCOUNTER A SETBACK, FAILURE OR defeat in sport or in life, how do you generally think about it? There are two perspectives or thinking styles I want you to consider.

The first is an optimistic thinking style, where you believe that the setback, failure or defeat is just temporary, that its causes are unique to a specific situation. You believe it is not your fault (you tend to not personalise it or blame yourself wholly for the setback): circumstances, bad luck or other people brought it about. Such people are unfazed by defeats. Confronted by a bad situation, they perceive it as a challenge and try harder.

The other style is the opposite. How have you approached or explained situations from a pessimistic perspective? The pessimist believes that bad events will last a long time or possibly forever (*permanent*), will undermine everything they do in all aspects of life (*pervasive*) and are their own fault (*personalise* blame, that the setback is down to me entirely). These are the three *p*s of a pessimist's thinking style.

Your thinking style has consequences. From hundreds of studies, Dr Martin Seligman in his book *Learned Optimism* shows how pessimists give up more easily and become depressed more often. He shows that optimists perform better in school, college, at work and in sporting pursuits. In addition, they age well, have better immune systems and are freer from physical illness in middle age. They even live longer.

The good news is that we can all learn how to be optimists – by using the power of 'non-negative thinking' and changing the destructive things we say to ourselves when we experience setbacks, defeats and losses.

In this chapter, we will learn how to develop this optimistic thinking style on a more consistent basis.

My journey to an optimistic thinking style

In 2012, Galway started a new campaign with new management. It followed the previous year's ten-point defeat to Waterford in the All-Ireland quarter-final, a defeat that negatively affected me for months afterwards. I felt extremely low, despondent and pessimistic that we were never going to win an All-Ireland. In the 2010 quarter-final against Tipperary, we'd had a two-point lead approaching the end of the match, and then conceded three points and lost by one in injury time. Tipperary went on to win the All-Ireland that year and denied Kilkenny the five-in-a-row. The Waterford defeat the following year felt like a huge step backwards.

And so, it was back to the drawing board with new management in the winter of 2011, my fourth new management team in eight years. In 2008, Ger Loughnane had brought in twenty Under-21 players to the group and some of the more experienced players were let go. It always made me angry to think that such experience was being lost. Although the Under-21s had been successful, and many of those players no doubt had potential, many of them were not ready physically, mentally or emotionally for the step up to senior hurling. There was no organised plan to help them – some of those players were lost to county hurling after a few weeks and never went back. A tragic loss of potential.

So, in the winter of 2011 when I saw over twenty Under-21 players coming in again, my thinking was quite pessimistic, that these changes would affect squad morale on and off the field for a long time (a quite permanent and pervasive perspective). It felt like déjà vu.

However, despite my pessimistic outlook, the pre-season went quite well with new gym and running programmes implemented, and the squad improved physically. We won our first couple of pre-season games quite well, before losing in the Walsh Cup in January to Kilkenny by 2–20 to 1–14. I felt extremely disappointed by our lack of performance, considering the work we had put in for twelve weeks and that Kilkenny were just back from holidays.

Once again, I questioned the quality of our squad to myself and bemoaned the loss of experienced inter-county players. I was finding it hard to see how we would be competitive that season. My thinking after the Kilkenny defeat was quite permanent and pervasive.

Galway's league campaign – from February to May 2012 – was inconsistent, and we needed to beat Kilkenny away in our last game to avoid a relegation play-off. Team selection was inconsistent throughout the league, and we were finding it hard to get our teamwork and patterns of play together. Kilkenny beat us by twenty-seven points, which only served to increase my pessimism.

I could see the younger players were trying hard, but the step up was proving difficult and it was taking us time to form into a cohesive team. I had got used to the panel we'd had for the previous three seasons, and the close bonds we'd built up on and off the field. I was twenty-eight years old and badly wanted success. My mindset was focused on many things outside my control, which heavily influenced how I felt, and my behaviours were not always supportive of management's ideas and changes.

In the short term, we had to beat Dublin to retain our Division One league status. In fairness to management, they remained optimistic in their communication. They were consistent that this was part of developing together as a team, that these were learning experiences that would help us grow. The factors that were leading to defeats were temporary, specific and external. We were learning how to become a team, and these were teething problems we needed to address in the short term to bring longer term success.

They were optimistic that, in time, all the younger players would bed in with the experienced players, that we had the ability and quality needed to be successful. We just had to keep working hard and stick together.

They listened to players' opinions and gave them a voice on what we needed to improve. This helped me personally, to share what I was feeling. Hearing the management's perspective on what they were trying to do meant I could reframe some of my pessimistic beliefs. In training, we started to see improvement in our sharpness, teamwork and confidence. We beat Dublin comprehensively after a replay, which gave us a good deal of confidence approaching the championship.

The attitude around the camp became far more positive. We were becoming more confident by the week that we would have a good championship run. We were now clearer on our roles and responsibilities and were sharing key knowledge with each other on how we were going to play.

We beat Westmeath and Offaly to reach the Leinster final. We were creating many chances, scoring well and our link-up play was very good. Our forwards and midfielders were working back to close space in our defence. Players were making selfless and unseen runs to help teammates. We were optimistic heading into the Leinster final against Kilkenny. We were injury-free, preparing well and in good form.

Approaching the final, nobody gave us much hope. Eight weeks previously, Kilkenny had beaten us by twenty-seven points and had won nine of the previous ten Leinster titles. Galway had never won one. We knew, though, that since that heavy defeat we were stronger, sharper and more cohesive, and had a strong belief in our ability individually and collectively. We knew our roles, our game plan and what we wanted to achieve. We were ready.

We dominated Kilkenny for most of the final. We held them scoreless for the first twenty minutes and ended up winning by eight points. The rest of the country was in shock, but we knew what we were capable of that day.

Recognising negative mindsets

To understand more about your thinking styles when you are faced with adversity, it is important to explore two key areas: learned helplessness and explanatory style.

Learned helplessness is the giving-up reaction to setbacks, the quitting response that follows from the belief that whatever you do doesn't matter or won't make a difference anyway. Explanatory style is the way in which we habitually explain to ourselves why events happen. An optimistic explanatory style is the medicine that stops helplessness, whereas a pessimistic explanatory style can be the poison that spreads it. The way you explain events to yourself determines how helpless you become or how energised (motivated to move forward and act) you are when you encounter everyday setbacks or big defeats. This is sometimes referred to as 'the word in your heart', for example 'Am I going to try again?' Is it a yes or no that your heart responds with?

At times during our 2012 season, I did momentarily slip into helpless mode when we were defeated. I told myself that the setup was the same as before, that replacing over half the panel was not the answer. To move forward, I had to break free from these habitual thoughts when setbacks happened.

How do you think about your setbacks? 'It's down to me, it's going to last forever, it's going to undermine everything I do' or 'It's just circumstances within this situation, it will pass soon, and, besides, there is much more to life than just this setback'?

Your habitual way of explaining setbacks is more than just the words you say when you fail. It is the habit of thought, learned in childhood and adolescence. We often repeat these thoughts frequently to ourselves – 'I am not good enough', 'I am incompetent', 'I am useless'. These types of thought, repeated over and over, form a belief that, in turn, influences how we feel and how we act. This explanatory style comes directly from how you perceive your place in the world – whether you think you are valuable and deserving, or worthless and hopeless. We covered empowering versus self-limiting beliefs in Chapter 1. This explanatory style, and the beliefs you hold about yourself, are the essence of an optimist or a pessimist.

Explanatory styles

There are three dimensions to your explanatory style – permanence, pervasiveness and personalisation.

Permanence

The first dimension includes people who give up easily and believe that the causes of the bad things that happen to them are *permanent*. Those who resist this helplessness believe the causes are *temporary*.

This is a key difference in thinking style between pessimism and optimism.

PERMANENT (PESSIMISTIC)	TEMPORARY (OPTIMISTIC)
I'm always tired.	I am tired today because of a bad night's sleep.
Training speed never works. I never get any faster.	Training speed can work with the right programme at the right time in the week. I am getting faster.
I always give out about my teammates.	I give out about my teammates when they don't put enough effort in.
The manager is harsh in his tone.	The manager is in a bad mood some days and can be tough on us when he feels we are not hitting our standards in training and games.
I never get positive feedback.	I didn't get positive feedback after my past two games because my performances were below my usual standards.
I always underperform in big games.	I haven't performed in periods of the bigger games because opponents tend to have good periods too.

When we think about bad events in terms of 'always' and 'never', we have a permanent, pessimistic style.

When we think in terms of 'sometimes' or 'lately', we have a temporary, optimistic style.

When we inevitably experience failure in school, sport or relationships, it can make us at least momentarily helpless. As former heavyweight world champion boxer Mike Tyson says, we all have a plan until we get punched in the face! It hurts to fail at something we care about.

For some, that hurt can dissipate quickly. For others, however, it lasts, and they can remain helpless for days or even months afterwards. This was something I struggled with in different ways. Losing a game in pre-season or league was easier to recover from because the next game was coming up fast and I hadn't time to ruminate on negative thoughts. We could often put these setbacks down to heavy training and winter hurling, not being championship sharp yet. The next session was a chance to work out some of the demons from that bad event. For the most part, I believed that we could win the next game, and it would reduce the impact of the previous loss.

If we lost a few games on the bounce in the championship or lost our last championship game, I tended to become very pessimistic, judging my performance with lots of 'always' and 'never'. Because it was the last game of championship for almost twelve months, it was easier to dwell on the negatives. Sometimes, my whole explanation of a season could be on losing the quarter-final and I would just disregard everything else we might have done during that season. When you play at senior level for ten years, you will inevitably suffer setbacks and could very easily adopt an unhealthy habitual pessimistic thinking style unknown to yourself.

From 2003 to 2013, we had six or seven crushing defeats, in quarter-finals in particular. I tended to explain these from a permanent, pervasive and personal perspective. I hadn't the tools or capacity at the time to correct this.

Optimistic and pessimistic outlook also applies when good things happen. People who believe good events have permanent causes are more optimistic than those who believe they have temporary causes.

TEMPORARY (PESSIMISTIC)	PERMANENT (OPTIMISTIC)
It was a lucky day.	I'm always lucky because I practise hard, and, more times than not, the shots come off in important games.
I tried hard.	I always try hard, and I am a committed player. I believe I have good ability. I always bring a positive attitude to situations and believe success is possible.
Luckily for me, my opponent got tired.	My opponent got tired because I always try to make smart runs and good decisions, and I am resilient during adversity. I mentally and physically wore them down.

Optimistic people explain good events to themselves in terms of permanence: traits, abilities and always. Pessimists name transient things: mood, effort and sometimes. Those who believe good events have permanent causes try even harder after they succeed. Those who see temporary reasons for good events may give up even when they succeed, believing success was a fluke.

Pervasiveness

The next dimension is pervasiveness. People who come up with universal explanations for their failures give up on everything when failure happens. Those who offer specific explanations may become helpless in that one part of their lives, yet more courageous in other areas.

UNIVERSAL (PESSIMISTIC)	SPECIFIC (OPTIMISTIC)
All coaches are unfair.	Our strength and conditioning coach is unfair for getting us to do conditioning runs after some games.
I'm not good enough.	I'm sometimes not good enough at speed endurance tests during the season.
Management teams are useless.	This management team is lacking when it comes to constructive feedback.
All opponents are too strong. Everyone is better than me at everything.	This opponent is tougher than most other opponents. When they are on form, they are very hard to beat.

The optimistic explanatory style for good events is the opposite to that for bad events. The optimist believes that bad events have specific causes, while good events will enhance everything he/she does; the pessimist believes that bad events have universal causes and that good events are because of specific factors.

SPECIFIC (PESSIMISTIC)	UNIVERSAL (OPTIMISTIC)
I'm good at tackling only. I am only good at sport.	I'm a good person and have lots of ability.
My coach knows some tactics for puckouts.	My coach knows the game inside out and has tactics for when we have the ball and when we don't have the ball.
I was welcoming to my new teammate on their first day.	I am a welcoming person.

Another factor that we must consider around optimism is hope. Whether or not we have hope depends on two aspects of our explanatory style: pervasiveness and permanence.

Finding temporary and specific causes for misfortune is the art of hope. Temporary causes limit helplessness in time, and specific causes limit helplessness to the original situation.

On the other hand, permanent causes produce helplessness far into the future, and universal causes spread helplessness throughout all our pursuits. Finding permanent and universal causes for misfortune is the practice of despair.

HOPELESS	HOPEFUL
I'm stupid.	I'm just tired today and found it harder to concentrate.
Coaches are always giving out.	My coach was just in a bad mood this morning. I will check in with him tomorrow to see how he is and ask for some feedback then.
There's a 9 out of 10 chance that this lump means my ACL is gone.	There's a 9 out of 10 chance that this lump is nothing, just some bruising from the contact in the tackle.

People who come up with permanent and universal explanations for their difficulties and setbacks tend to collapse under pressure, both for a long time and across situations. That's why moving from pessimism to optimism is so important, be it in sport, health, career, leadership or relationships.

Personalisation: internal versus external
The final dimension to discuss is personalisation. When bad things happen, we can blame ourselves (internalise) or we can blame other people or circumstances (externalise).

- People who blame themselves when they fail can have low self-esteem consequently. They think they are worthless, talentless and unlovable.
- People who blame external events do not lose self-esteem when bad things happen. Overall, they like themselves better than those who blame themselves.

INTERNAL (LOW SELF-ESTEEM)	EXTERNAL (HIGH SELF-ESTEEM)
I'm stupid.	We are all stupid on different subject matters. No one can be an expert at everything!
I have no talent at soccer.	I have no luck at soccer sometimes.
I'm insecure.	I grew up in poverty.

An important thing to remember is that personalisation controls only how you feel about yourself. Pervasiveness and permanence control what you do: how long you remain helpless and across how many situations. Personalisation is the only one that is easy to fake; we can blame our troubles on others quite easily.

Another important thing to note is that the optimistic style of explaining good events is the inverse to that for bad events: it's internal rather than external. People who believe they cause good things to happen tend to like themselves better than those who believe good things come from other people or circumstances.

EXTERNAL (PESSIMISTIC)	INTERNAL (OPTIMISTIC)
A stroke of luck.	I can take advantage of luck.
My teammates' skill won us that game.	My skill helps me make good decisions under pressure. I am blessed to be skilful at sport.
The opponents didn't play well today, that is why we weren't hammered.	We performed well today in terms of our effort, teamwork and skill execution. That is why we pushed them all the way.

But is it right that I should blame others for my failures? It is clear, we want to take responsibility, and we want to be able to change. If we want to change, internality is not as crucial as permanence.

If we believe the cause is permanent – stupidity, lack of talent, appearance – we will not act to change or improve ourselves. If we believe the cause is temporary – a bad mood, too little effort, lack of fitness – we can act to change it.

If we want to be responsible for what we do, then, yes, we want to have an internal style. More importantly, we must have a temporary style for bad events – we must believe that whatever the cause of that bad event, it can be changed. We have the power to affect our future with what we do now.

What if you are a pessimist?

If your explanatory style is pessimistic, you may encounter trouble in four main areas:

- You are more susceptible to depression.
- You are potentially achieving less at work than your talents warrant.
- Your physical health and your immune function are probably not where they should be, and this may get worse as you get older. Therefore, you are potentially more susceptible to illness and injury.
- Your life is not as pleasurable as it should be. Pessimistic explanatory style is a misery.

In times of crisis, you may be knocked flat by your setbacks and struggle to cope for weeks and months. You are not going to get the best from your talents in sport, career or life with this pessimistic style. When you get injured, it will take you longer to recover. When you lose a match, it will take you longer to move towards positive effort and training habits. Over the course of a career, you could miss out on many weeks of preparation and enjoyment of your sport and life because of this negative habitual thinking style.

Mental training

It is important to reaffirm that it is possible to move from pessimism to optimism. We can learn the skills of an optimist. The five points given below are a good starting point for you to unpack your thinking style around setbacks, defeats and failures.

1. Learn to recognise the automatic thoughts that go through your consciousness when you are at a low ebb. These are often referred to as ANTs (automatic negative thoughts) – quick phrases or sentences that are well practised. They can often go unnoticed and unchallenged. Learn to become aware of these assumptions, judgements and explanations that drive us into a negative state. They are often permanent, pervasive and personal explanations. In sport, they might sound like: 'I'm terrible – I am performing worse and worse each year. I am always such a failure at everything I do.'

2. Learn to challenge the ANTs by looking for contrary evidence. What do you do well at – be it sport, career, relationships, lifestyle? Examples in sport might be: 'I am fit and can get up and down the field quite easily. I am very good at covering back and reading danger. I am an accurate passer. I can score when I get into the right positions.' You focus on this evidence and see that it contradicts the previous negativity of being 'terrible and always a failure at everything'.

3. Use different explanations, called reattributions, to challenge your automatic negative thoughts. For example: 'I'm quite good at certain things like covering back, reading danger, passing and shooting.' Change 'I am useless at tackling' to 'I am good at

stopping my opponent when in close – I can use my strength to hold him up' and 'When she runs at me, I can get better at moving my feet and getting hands on her to slow down her momentum – I will work on my footwork in training until I get better'.

4. Learn how to divert yourself from negative thoughts. You can use the skills we have already discussed, such as focusing on breathing, speaking out loud to yourself with positive or instructional self-talk or affirmations, being mindful in what you're doing in the moment or using the image in your mind of a stop sign to break the negative thinking habit.
5. Learn to recognise and question the negative assumptions governing so much of what you do: this might mean moving from 'Everything I do must be perfect or I'm a failure' to 'Success is putting my best effort in and, regardless of the outcome, I am okay'. Or changing 'I need everyone to like me, or I have failed' to 'I don't need anyone's approval. I accept myself with all my strengths and limitations – everyone has flaws, there is no perfect human being'.

So, when we fail at something, we become helpless and depressed, at least momentarily. We don't initiate action as quickly as we would otherwise, or we may not try at all. If we do try, we will not persist.

Our explanatory style is the great modulator of learned helplessness. Optimists recover from their momentary helplessness immediately. Very soon after failing, they pick themselves up and start again. For them, defeat is a challenge, a mere setback on the road to inevitable success. They see defeat as temporary and specific, not pervasive.

Pessimists tend to wallow in defeat, which they view as permanent and pervasive. They can become depressed and stay helpless for long periods. A setback is a defeat, and they often view one defeat as the loss of the war. They don't try again for weeks or months, if at all. If they do try, the slightest new setback throws them back into a helpless state again.

Success will not necessarily go to the most talented. The medals and trophies will go to the adequately talented who are optimists.

What are the predictions around sport for having an optimistic explanatory style?

Those with the most optimistic explanatory style will go on to win. They will win because they will try harder, particularly after a defeat or under tough challenges. The same thing is true for teams. If a team can be characterised by its level of optimism, the more optimistic team will win more often, if talent is equal, and this will be most apparent under pressure.

When athletes' explanatory style is changed from pessimistic to optimistic, they win more, particularly under pressure. Roger Federer recently gave the example that he loses 43 per cent of the points in a match – this goes to show how important it is for him to view these point losses as temporary and specific to that moment. If he personalised those mistakes and saw them as a lack of ability, I doubt his record would be as good as it is, and his career would not have lasted as long as it did.

In relation to explanatory style, ask yourself the following:

1. Do I get discouraged easily?
2. Do I get depressed easily more than I want to?
3. Do I fail more than I think I should?

If your answer is yes to any of these questions, you have skills to learn around optimistic explanatory style.

You can deploy these optimism skills in how you talk to yourself in many scenarios:

- In an achievement situation (such as winning a game, getting a new job, presenting a proposal to new clients).
- If you are concerned about how you feel (struggling with a low mood).
- If you want to lead and inspire others.
- If a situation is going to take time and your physical health is an issue (overcoming an injury in sport, not making an inter-county panel).

However, do not use optimism if your goal is to plan for a risky and uncertain future or if you are counselling others whose future is dim or if you want to appear sympathetic to the troubles of others – do not begin with optimism, although using it later, once confidence and empathy are established, may help.

The fundamental guideline is to ask, for any situation, what the cost of failure is. If the cost is high, optimism is the wrong strategy. The sports person trying a new skill, a new position or trying to win a game generally risks frustration, not life and limb. These are low-risk failures, and we should use optimism for these scenarios.

Training steps: on the pitch

When we encounter adversity, we react by thinking about it. Our thoughts form into beliefs. These beliefs may become so habitual that we don't even realise we have them unless we stop and focus on them. These beliefs have consequences for us; they are the direct causes of what we feel and what we do next. They can be the difference between giving up or taking constructive action.

You can use the acronym ABCDE to help you identify the different setbacks you face (*adversity*), what you think after these events (your *beliefs*) how you feel and behave (the *consequences*), how you push back against negative thoughts (*disputing your beliefs*) and how you engage with your feelings (*energisation*). Disputing your beliefs is giving your disturbing beliefs an argument. By disputing them in an effective way (see the four main elements on the next page) we can move from dejection and giving up to more positive action. Try to come up with as many alternatives and evidence to dispute your irrational belief as if you were going to court. Energisation is noticing how you feel when you dispute this irrational belief and truly believe the counter arguments and alternatives. These tools are important for coaches and players to develop throughout the season to move on from momentary helplessness and depression after the inevitable setbacks occur.

There are four main elements to effective disputation.

1. **Evidence** What is the evidence both for and against the belief? Often, we catastrophise by jumping to the worst possible conclusion in the absence of solid evidence – sometimes on the smallest hunches, as our brain is lazy and biased and takes mental shortcuts to find answers as fast as possible.
2. **Alternatives** Is there any other way to look at the adversity? Start to generate some alternatives and scan the evidence for each one.
3. **Implications** What if your dark explanation is right? Is it the end of the world? Just because a situation is unfavourable doesn't mean it's necessarily a catastrophe. Develop the important skill of de-catastrophising by examining the situation's most realistic implications.
4. **Usefulness** Sometimes, the accuracy of your explanation is not what really matters. What matters is whether thinking about the issue now will do any good. Will sulking or brooding over getting dropped from the team help you now? When we notice ourselves brooding and going into a low mood, we can distract ourselves by doing something physical, such as snapping a wrist band and repeating the word 'stop' to ourselves or immersing ourselves in cold water, such as a shower, ice bath or the sea. You can schedule a specific time for thinking things over regarding the issue. Write down any troublesome thoughts you are having about not getting selected the moment they occur. You can then return to them at your specific time, so brooding is no longer mentally necessary.

We get many opportunities through sport to practise overcoming setbacks and to try harder when the next opportunity presents itself. Adversities that teams and individuals face include selection issues, injury issues, conflict with team members and defeat. Using the following examples as a guide, try to think of adversity events that could derail or disrupt you during the season. Implementing the ABCDEs – adversity, beliefs, consequences, disputing and energisation – to frame how you have reacted previously is a useful way to build awareness of our habitual thinking in such scenarios.

- **Adversity** I lose a game.
- **Belief** I played poorly. I let my teammates down. What is the point of all this hard work when I perform like that? I feel so embarrassed.
- **Consequence** I get angry and withdraw from others for a few days. I don't feel motivated to do anything. I feel worthless.
- **Disputing your beliefs** My whole performance was not poor. When I looked back at the match, I saw that I had lots of possession, I used it well, I created four scoring chances. I took two scores myself – nearly 40 per cent of our first-half scores. My man was switched off me after twenty-five minutes because of the amount of ball I was winning. My teammates were not let down by me. I gave it my all. It was my first game back in eight months. I was quite surprised at my sharpness and fitness after only a few weeks' training. I am only going to improve with more sessions, games and learning from what I did well.

- **Energisation** From disputing my beliefs, I now feel confident in my first-half performance. I just tired a bit in the second half from lack of match practice, but I will get stronger in the coming weeks.

- **Adversity** There is a lack of commitment from teammates.
- **Belief** They don't really care, they are not ambitious like me. They are not great teammates and show poor leadership. I feel frustrated playing with them.
- **Consequence** I pull back sometimes from building close relationships with them and from finding out what challenges they face week to week to commit to the team.
- **Disputing your beliefs** They do care. Most of them are playing two codes, different age groups and are combining this with study or work. There are huge demands on them, and from my own experience it is hard to balance all these things and still have quality time with friends and family. They are committed and do a lot of training and are ambitious on and off the field
- **Energisation** I will work harder at appreciating the individual qualities and effort my teammates bring and will find out more about the challenges they face week to week.

There are challenges we face each day regarding preparation (sleep, nutrition, hydration, meditation, goal-setting, time management, motivation, financial pressure, etc.), training (traffic, work deadlines, relationship stressors, gym exercises, warm-ups, preventative work or tackling, running or defending drills) or match-day routines (eating, nerves, other people's opinions, delays to the schedule, refereeing decisions, intimidation from opposition, disagreements with team members, etc.) or perhaps speaking with teammates or management when not selected.

When you have recorded five ABC situations, look over your beliefs carefully. You will probably see how pessimistic explanations have set off passivity and dejection, whereas optimistic explanations set off activity. So now our next step is to change your habitual pessimistic explanations that are set off by adversities. We can do this by disputing some of the thoughts and feelings that surround these adversities.

When something bad happens, you must break out of your low mood by disputing pessimistic explanations. When our beliefs are formed based on negativity and pessimism, it is important that we challenge them as soon as possible.

After working through these disputations, you must focus on externalising them – bringing your thoughts out into the open where they can be dealt with. Choose someone you trust to practise with. Their job is to put to you any pessimistic criticism that you might put on yourself. Go over your ABCDE record with them, so they can see what kind of criticism you routinely attack yourself with. Your job is to dispute the criticisms out loud, using every argument and evidence you can come up with.

It is not always easy to adopt an optimistic thinking style. You have probably been in situations where optimistic thinking has not always helped. For example, after failing an exam or job interview or losing a match, where you underperformed and felt sick with disappointment. People telling you not to worry, that there is always next time or that you can enjoy some time off now or that the team was unlucky after a ten-point drubbing only serves to leave you feeling empty, ashamed and embarrassed.

What I have found is that when in this negative mindset, it can be very hard to adopt the optimistic thinking style that focuses on the opportunity from a situation. What is the valuable lesson? What is the new task to be accomplished?

It is not always easy to go from deeply intense negative feelings to positive feelings. You must first find some neutral ground – and, to get there, you must find a way to navigate the discomfort of these negative feelings.

Is it high-energy negative feelings like anger, envy and frustration? Is it low-energy negative feelings like embarrassment, guilt and disappointment? Which do you think are healthy feelings and which unhealthy? Is anger an unhealthy feeling? Is frustration a healthier counterpart?

If you are not used to talking about how you are feeling, it can be quite hard to find the words to reflect your feelings.

Exercise

BUILDING EMOTIONAL AWARENESS AND SPACE
Following is an exercise you might find useful. Think of a time when you experienced a setback, be it losing a match, failing an exam or having a disagreement with someone. Try to put into words some

of the feelings you were experiencing. Circle some of the words (feelings) in the table that resonated with how you felt afterwards. Then, rank them from one to five in terms of intensity.

FEELING	OTHER FORMS OF THIS FEELING
Angry	Aggressive, annoyed, irritated, furious, fuming, touchy, resentful, cross, complaining, enraged, bad-tempered, livid
Anxious	Edgy, fearful, apprehensive, frightened, nervous, panicky, restless, tense, uneasy, bothered, worried, concerned
Ashamed	Belittled, degraded, discredited, disgraced, humiliated, mortified, vilified, dishonoured
Disappointed	Deflated, dejected, discouraged, disheartened, disillusioned, gutted, let down, crestfallen
Embarrassed	Awkward, humiliated, diminished, insecure, self-conscious, small, timid, weak, unsure, uncertain, unconfident, uncomfortable
Envious	Sour, spiteful, malicious, green with envy
Guilty	At fault, indefensible, inexcusable, unforgivable, in the wrong, condemned, culpable
Hurt	Broken-hearted, cut up, cut to the quick, devastated, damaged, gutted, hard done by, harmed, offended, wounded, pained, injured, aggrieved
Jealous	Bitter, doubtful, distrustful, sceptical, suspicious, wary
Sad	Blue, distraught, distressed, down, shattered, sorrowful, tearful, inconsolable, downhearted

When you can recognise the feeling and name it, write it down and explain what happened. This can help you to create some space and separation from the emotion and the situation you have been in. This allows you to lessen the power that feeling has over you.

Start to validate these feelings. It is okay to feel this way: you worked hard and wanted to be successful. It really hurts when something you care about and worked hard for doesn't happen how you would have liked.

It can be useful to write down your healthy and unhealthy feelings. It can help you to understand your thinking in these situations. If you recognise that you are experiencing an uncomfortable feeling, you can challenge any faulty thinking that might be leading to your unhealthy emotional responses.

Remember, it is never the situation that causes you to feel angry. Anger comes from inside you. So, it is the thoughts you are generating about the situation that are causing you to feel angry. If you can observe what the thoughts are, you can begin to recognise the unhelpful illusion you have created around the situation in question. You might have assumed, 'I shouldn't have lost that match'. But have any of us a right to succeed in any match? So, it is the thought that has generated this unhelpful emotion of anger. You can now choose to reframe the thought or let it pass through without giving it anymore energy or attention.

Pursue the positive

The positive psychology view of the world is that learned optimism is a strategy you can harness and practise. The human mind is an amazing processing tool. We have the ability, through our subconscious mind, to absorb twenty million pieces of information per second. The conscious mind, on the other hand, tends to focus on between seven and forty pieces of information. This is referred to as a 'mental shortcut'. These shortcuts are designed to help us make judgements quickly, so we do not have sensory overload.

You arrive at a coffee shop and there are twenty options for coffee and teas and another forty different pastry options. You are thinking about trying something new. The pressure builds as you're about to order. What to choose! What to quickly disqualify! When we are judging situations quickly, we often fail to see the bigger picture and we choose the easiest, familiar and fastest route, even if it is unhelpful. So, you pick the familiar flat white and croissant!

Below are some common shortcuts we take.

1. **Jumping to conclusions** You finish training, and you see your manager's name pop up on your phone. You automatically think he is going to criticise you or drop you from the team. Judging a situation based on assumptions, rather than relying on the facts, is jumping to conclusions.
2. **Mental filtering** The game is over. Your team has won. Supporters are coming onto the field and praising you for your contribution and how well you played. One supporter mentions the ball you dropped in the first half that led to a score against the team. All you hear is *that* comment – you discount everything else that is said. You should have held that ball and you are always dropping high balls. When you pay attention to the negative feedback (even when there is positive), that is mental filtering.

3. **Magnifying** The game is due to start in a few minutes. The biggest crowd of the year is expected. It is announced that the game has been put back fifteen minutes to let the supporters in. 'Why is this happening? I am ready to play now. This is typical of the organisers – why don't they open more entrances? Why do I have to be punished with the game starting later?' That's magnifying – when you search for and focus on the negative aspects in a situation.

4. **Minimising** You have got your game stats back. You have hit your highest possessions, tackles and pass completion rates of the year so far. Your free concession count, however, was one higher than usual. Your coaches are really pleased with your contribution and tell you it was your most consistent game so far this year. Everyone is pleased for you, but all you can focus on is the extra foul you gave away. Minimising is when you dismiss the positive aspects of a situation.

5. **Personalising** You are analysing the game with one of the coaches and fellow defenders. The coach praises a young defender for how hard he has worked over the past few weeks and how this hard work, along with his good form in training, is why he played well. You have felt tired the past week or two and have not been able to train as hard. You feel that this is a direct dig at your efforts, that the coach thinks you're not hard-working. Personalising is when you believe that everything others do, or say, is somehow directed at you.

6. **Blaming** You are not selected for a particular game. The coach tells you that, in recent weeks, your form and commitment have

dipped. You tell people that the coach hasn't a clue and doesn't believe in you. Blaming is putting responsibility on someone else, so you don't have to solve your own problems. It's denying that you are in control of your own behaviour, feelings and actions.

7. **Over-generalising** Over the past few years, to improve your speed, you have done a yoga session every week and a new gym programme and you changed your diet. But it didn't work; you are still getting beaten for pace when someone runs hard at you. So, you give up on the yoga, the gym and the nutrition and tell yourself that you will never be fast enough. See the danger in that? It's not atypical to experience setbacks in life, but when we choose to hang on to them, it's likely that those negative thoughts will become our forever truth.

8. **Emotional reasoning** The position of team captain has become vacant. You have been on the team for the past seven years and have displayed excellent leadership qualities. You are valued by the coaches and players for your contributions on and off the field. But you believe, for some reason, that you would never be considered for this position. You feel unworthy, and that a newcomer would be better suited to the role. Emotional reasoning is when your reaction to something defines your reality, that how you feel about something makes it true for you, no matter how illogical it might be.

How do you stop irrational thinking?

Though they may seem overwhelming, these thoughts are normal. As we have discussed, our old brains have traditionally been on the lookout for threats. Over time, we have evolved to look out for issues, to solve them and to learn from our mistakes. The challenge with this is that becoming good at identifying problems strengthens our negative thinking habits. We make quick judgements on things, based on our core beliefs about ourselves, others and the world – and, sometimes, these judgements or distortions fail to see the full picture.

You are programmed to have automatic negative thoughts, but that does not mean that these automatic negative thoughts are fixed. You can change the programme by altering your beliefs and thinking styles. You can alter your views on anything, but you must first understand how pessimistic thinking styles develop.

1. **Attention and information processing** Your brain's threat-detection system is naturally scanning for danger to protect you and keep you safe.

    You see a substitute warming up during the game and you think that you are going to be taken off. You disregard the fact that subs warm up every five minutes, usually in case of an injury in their position. As a pessimist, you filter out the positive cues and focus on negative ones. The optimistic thinking style would say that this is part of our game routine. It is great to see everyone tuned in. Now, bring your attention back to what's in your control and return to the task at hand.

2. **Locus of control** This is the belief that you can change or control elements of your life, that you are an agent in your success and play an active role in it.

In a sporting context, you might not have started the last game. Optimistic thinking would say: 'If I put together a few good sessions and keep showing good form, I will give myself a great opportunity to be selected.' Pessimistic thinking, on the other hand, would be: 'No matter what I do, it won't be enough. I will never get a game again.' After a setback, do you have an internal or an external locus of control?

INTERNAL LOCUS OF CONTROL	EXTERNAL LOCUS OF CONTROL
• You have a strong belief that you can influence events and their outcomes. • You attribute results to your own skills and ability. • You believe events in life come primarily from your own actions. • When you fail, you put it down to poor effort or strategy.	• You have a strong belief that you have little influence over events or their outcomes. • You attribute results to task complexity or luck. • You believe that events in life happen primarily outside of your own actions. • When you fail, you put it down to your lack of ability or because the task is too hard.

On the pitch

Players on a bus heading for Croke Park on All-Ireland final day can be engaged in a variety of thinking styles. Those who are starting might believe in their ability and skills to perform, that positive outcomes can and will happen. Other players might be sitting on negative thoughts, that their ability and skill levels may not be up to it, that things could go wrong. Others could be in a neutral place, present and engaged in the conversations and what they are doing right now. It is very normal to be moving through this continuum of past-, present- or future-based thinking, feeling, imagery and behaving.

It's 12 February 2022, and Harry and Tim were seated on the bus together heading to Croke Park for the biggest day in the club calendar, All-Ireland club final day. Ballygunner were facing the record-holders Ballyhale in that year's decider.

Tim had been out all season with a cruciate injury and had been helping the backroom team on match days with stats and other key information. He had been at every team meeting, training session and match even though he was not able to play any part on the field. He had been a total team player and great teammate, always looking at how best he could serve the team.

Tim knew that doubts could begin to surface for players on these journeys before matches. He decided to share with his teammate Harry what he had seen in him over the previous few weeks. How good his attitude and form had been in training. How ready and capable he was to make an impact today.

Harry has a natural optimistic thinking style and even though he was not starting he fully believed he was going to have an impact that day in the game. Tim's reinforcement of his positive qualities would have further reinforced those empowering positive thoughts that are needed to succeed on big days. When and if he was called on, he would make a big impact on the game. Harry had not played in the semi-final. His last competitive championship outing had been fifteen minutes in the Munster final three months earlier. He had no prior experience of All-

Ireland final day. His optimistic thinking style about his ability, his positive attitude and the preparation he had gone through filled every inch of his being. He believed he was going to influence the team's performance in the final through his actions, that the day would be a great experience. He came on in the last fifteen minutes and had a huge impact, scoring the winning goal in injury time, helping the team to create history and win their first All-Ireland.

Our thoughts can help change our lives!

Mental training

How can you lean into a more optimistic, open and flexible view of things? What practices can you develop that will move you towards this more optimistic thinking style? The following exercises will help.

Exercises

EXERCISE 1: RECALL

When was the last time your optimistic thinking style was in operation? Please take some time to write out some of your reflections on the questions below:

- When in the past did you expect good things to happen and an event to turn out positively for you?
- Who was there?
- Can you recall what you were thinking before the event?
- What were you focused on?

- What were you feeling?
- What were your behaviours that day?
- How did you feel during and after the event?
- What did you learn from the experience?

Contrast that with a more pessimistic style of thinking.
- When in the past did you expect bad things to happen and an event to turn out negatively for you?
- Who was there?
- Can you recall what you were thinking before the event?
- What were you focused on?
- What were you feeling?
- What were your behaviours that day?
- How did you feel during and after the event?
- What did you learn from the experience?

EXERCISE 2: THE POWER TO CHOOSE

We can choose how we approach obstacles or difficult experiences. With challenges or setbacks, we should consider this process of evaluation:

- **Adversity** What is the obstacle or setback that you are facing?
- **Belief** What is your perception of the obstacle or setback? Is it temporary? Is it specific to this context? Are there external factors at play? What is in your control regarding this situation?
- **Consequence** What is the resulting action or reaction to the obstacle or setback based on your perception?

EXERCISE 3: MARTIN SELIGMAN'S FOUR-STEP GUIDE TO FACING CHALLENGING SITUATIONS

When facing an upcoming event or situation, try to identify the things that will enable you to lean into the challenge in a more positive way.

- **Evidence** What are the facts of the situation, and do they support or contradict your perceptions?
- **Alternatives** Pessimists tend to latch on to the negative explanations for setbacks, often ignoring the more positive.
- **Implications** Pessimists tend to jump from negative implications to progressively more catastrophic ones, but what are the chances of these things happening?
- **Usefulness** Just because a belief is true doesn't mean it's useful. Clinging to useless beliefs keeps us from working on the things we can change about ourselves or the situation.

EXERCISE 4: THREE ATTITUDES OF AN OPTIMIST

Martyn Newman, a clinical psychologist and leading authority on emotional intelligence, outlines in his book *Emotional Capitalists* the three attitudes of an optimist.

- **Opportunity sensing** Optimistic leaders have a vision for where they are going. In times of change, they see the potential opportunities that they can take advantage of.
- **Positive mood** Optimistic leaders can harness and maintain a positive mood.

- **Resilience** The essence of resilience is to see a benefit in every situation, especially when there are setbacks. It's to seek the valuable lesson in any issue and to focus on the task to be accomplished, rather than on negative emotions such as disappointment or fear.

Consider something that has had a negative impact on your performance, and then apply the strategies of an optimist to see what happens.

Summary

Having an open, flexible and optimistic thinking style helps to positively influence our performances and outcomes, be it in sport, career, education, health, relationships or other areas. You too can learn to develop this optimistic thinking style; you can approach situations expecting positive things to happen.

As we have seen, you can learn to view your setbacks, defeats and failures from a more temporary, specific or universal perspective to help you recover faster, be more resilient and try harder in your preparation and in your future performances.

It is natural after several setbacks to fall into a pessimistic thinking style and to attribute the failure to your lack of ability. That you are useless. That you can never perform in these scenarios. That no matter how hard you try, you have little influence on the results. With your bad luck, how could you be successful?

Well, your pessimistic thinking tendency, for the most part, made you think and feel this way. It is time to take back some of your power and control. To focus on the attitude, skills, behaviours and effort you can use to be successful. To know that you can influence your next situation. That failing last time was not just down to you. You are not useless at everything just because you failed at this thing. You can be successful with the right attitude, effort and strategy.

We all experience setbacks at some stage. How you explain your setbacks to yourself has a major influence on your beliefs and subsequent actions. Understanding your explanatory style when approaching situations is critical. Understanding what is internal or external, stable or unstable, global or specific will help accelerate your chances of succeeding.

By reframing your locus of control (from external to internal) to what is in your control and power, by explaining setbacks in a healthier way, you can begin to open your lens of thinking and see a more optimistic thinking style appear. From here, you can harness your natural positive energy to achieve better performances and outcomes.

You will notice your tendency to focus on the opportunity rather than the problem. You will see situations as experiences to learn from. You will begin to focus on the controllable tasks to be accomplished.

8

INTENSITY VERSUS RECOVERY

IN PURSUING SUCCESS, IN WANTING TO IMPROVE and become the best at what you do, there is another vital component you must consider. Getting faster, stronger, fitter, more skilful, stronger mentally, more resilient are all important, but there is one component that makes each of those areas grow – energy.

If I have high amounts of positive energy in my life, then I start to gain real momentum in the areas that matter to me. The opposite is also true. You know what it's like to be depleted in energy, feeling lethargic in your movements, finding it hard to take in information, noticing your reactions are slow on the field.

If you are low in energy consistently, it is likely you are on the edge of doing too much.

When you are pursuing a goal that's very important to you, it's easy to fall into the trap of doing more and more. It is unusual to encounter a high performer in sport, business or life who feels they are doing enough to be successful. 'I need to get stronger', 'I need to train more', 'I should be fitter', 'I have to perform better', I want to be more confident', 'I need to be more consistent' are some of the comments I regularly hear when coaching people. Very often, I observe people working extremely hard, bringing high levels of intensity to their training and matches and doing extra sessions, such as gym, running, skills, recovery, analysis, etc. They often source most of their confidence from their preparation. They feel by always doing something physical, they are getting closer to their goal. They have linked working hard with being successful.

But what is the effect over time of always being in this high-intensity mode? When I am always switched on in this way, how does it affect my health, my well-being, my relationships and my performance? Is it possible to have consistent and repeatedly high-level performances? Is it healthy to always be striving, wanting, desiring something external?

If the answer is no, what does a healthy balance look and feel like from a mental, physical, emotional and spiritual perspective? What does feeling fresh and energised feel like?

In this chapter, I will explore why it is so important to balance short bursts of intensity with optimal recovery.

My journey to balancing intensity with recovery

In the early part of my Galway career, from 2003 to 2008, overtraining and under-recovering was an area I really struggled with. At that time, we didn't have access to GPS systems or wellness apps. Player welfare was not as advanced or well managed. We also did not have the education around training loads, stress and recovery that are available now. We did not have the awareness of the benefits of nutrition, sleep routines and recovery protocols.

During this time, I was juggling commitments between Under-21 level and senior inter-county hurling, and I was also playing colleges hurling. And I was playing Under-21 and intermediate with the club, and interprovincial hurling with Connacht. So, during the year, I could be involved in as many as six different teams, with different management and players and with many different expectations.

I was working part-time and studying for exams. I was trying to keep good relationships with friends and family but was struggling to see them. When I did have some free time, we were advised to rest up for the next training or game, but it often felt like there was another team session to attend or a gym session to complete. Days off rarely happened. I often felt I wasn't in control of my schedule or my time.

The break from the senior county setup in 2009 gave me breathing space to consider all these aspects of my life. I had also finished college and had become over age for Under-21 hurling, so this freed me up mentally and physically. I went from six teams in a season to just two.

This enabled me to take a fresh look at what I wanted from my hurling career. I knew that if I wanted to get back into the Galway senior setup, I would need better planning and organisation. Previously when I had a dip in form, I trained harder, longer and more often. I thought that to feel confident and get better, I needed to train more and more – but this only served to lessen my energy, enjoyment and performance levels.

I decided that when I got back on the panel, I was going to trust the training plan we had set out for us. The individual work I would do would be shorter, sharper and suited to what I needed. I reduced the time I spent in the gym, alleys or pitch on my nights off. I saw more of friends and family; I socialised more.

I felt more in control of my time, and my mood was calmer and more balanced. I began to sleep better. I began to eat more healthily, at more regular times. I found spending this time with teammates, friends and family improved my energy. Consequently, my game improved. I felt mentally sharper and physically more energised than ever before. I was finishing training and games very strongly. I felt motivated for my sessions. The more balanced approach to training and recovery really worked.

Feeling burned out

It is very normal to want and desire something. To strive to be successful at something you love and are passionate about is a wonderful ambition to foster. It helps you to get out of bed, focus on the task at hand and work hard, to have a sense of purpose and direction. It enables you to demonstrate what matters to you, what you stand for and what you believe in. Sport can enable people to show some of their greatest skills and character traits, such as commitment, persistence, tenacity and accountability.

Life is full of opportunities. You are in control of what you desire – a medal, a house, financial freedom, to be something in your life. Those ambitions give you motivation to get up early, to work hard and be healthy. Sometimes, when you are in that striving mode, it can feel very exciting. You get a buzz of adrenaline by working hard at getting closer to your dream. When you make progress, you produce dopamine, the reward hormone, which makes you feel alive.

But what happens when you are not making progress?

How do you feel when you are working hard for something you desire, and it feels almost impossible to reach? Have you felt stuck at some point in your life? Have you felt helpless and hopeless at the impossibility of it all? Have you felt drained of motivation and energy? Have you felt no desire to do it anymore? Have you felt stressed out at even the thought of doing an activity related to it?

It is easy to make assumptions when you see some highly skilled people perform in high-pressure situations. It is easy to assume they're 'natural', they're 'gifted', they're a 'once-in-a-generation' player – as if they were just born that way, naturally composed and confident.

This pedestal-pitching is not doing you or them any good. Some people may be born with a small amount of talent, but without effort, learning and training, they will never reach their full potential. The idol you admire got there by having the same challenging thoughts that you have, and by putting in the sweat and tears. They also frequently struggled for energy, motivation and intensity. They too have similar feelings of being stuck, helpless and hopeless when they see a lack of progress, even after many years at the top.

What elite sports people have learned to do better is accept that self-doubt and worry are part of the journey. No one goes through challenges without some doubt or fear. When we harness this intensity in the right way, we can focus more deeply on the work that is required. Elite performers know how to get this balance between consistent short bursts of intensity and optimal recovery right, and this solidifies the learnings in the brain, body and mind.

Shift out of stress

A useful theory to understand stress and its relationship to performance is the Yerkes–Dodson law, created by psychologists Robert M. Yerkes and John Dillingham Dodson in 1908. Very often stress has negative connotations, but, in fact, it is a stimulus, resulting in a positive or negative response to a specific situation.

- **Eustress** is the positive form of stress and gives a sense of arousal (psychological state of alertness and anticipation that prepares the body for action) and fulfilment.
- **Distress** is the negative form and can lead to panic, overwhelm and anxiety.

A negative response to a stressor may result in physiological changes, such as sweaty palms, racing heart and frequent visits to the toilet.

You may mentally predict that things will go wrong and experience psychological effects, such as panic, overwhelm and anxiety. This happens when you feel that you do not have the ability to cope with the demands that are placed on you.

When you feel you can cope with the stressor, you begin to move to a place of excitement and challenge, and you take positive action. This is a facilitative response to stress.

What helps you to cope with that demand are your own resources. These include:

1. **Self-belief** For example, that you have the skills to execute the task. Identifying previous experiences when you did them well is a great source of reassurance in pressure situations.
2. **Perception of control** For example, identifying exactly what you can control about the situation and what you can't. If you are a penalty-taker you are not 100 per cent in control of scoring, but you can control your breathing, and this will influence how you feel. You can direct your attention on the target you want to hit. You can direct your thoughts on technical or positive cues when lifting or hitting the ball as part of your routine.
3. **Achievement motivation** For example, focusing on specific task-related actions to complete the goal. Putting the right level of effort into your swing, being present in the moment, being positive in your self-talk: 'I can and will hit this ball into the corner.'
4. **Ability to redefine failure and what it means to you** Failing is the first attempt in learning. Without stretching and making mistakes, there is no growth. For example, 'This pressure I am

feeling is a privilege. I know I am expanding my potential. I am edging towards greatness.' Identifying what failure truly means to you and redefining that meaning if it affects you negatively in the key moments is important in managing your intensity.

Identifying your own optimal zones of stress

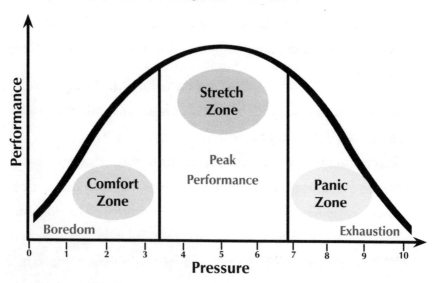

When you wake up in the morning, you may feel inactive, unmotivated or relaxed. This is an important zone to be in each day. It is beneficial to your recovery. This is often referred to as your 'comfort zone' and might fall between 0 and 3 on the pressure/stress scale out of ten, as seen in the graph adapted from the Yerkes–Dodson law.

As the day progresses, your stress curve may start to rise with getting to work or college on time, key client meetings, project deadlines, etc. You may move into your peak performance zone to motivate yourself in the direction you want to complete key tasks. This can also be called the 'stretch' or 'challenge zone' and falls between 4 and 6 on the pressure/stress scale out of ten.

If at some point during the day you are in a situation where the demand is too high, you slip into the third zone, which feels like panic, overwhelm and exhaustion if you are there too long. This might be called the panic zone. This falls between 7 and 10 on the pressure/stress scale out of ten. Think about the questions below and look at the examples in the table in relation to your own experience:

- Which activities do you like to do each day that put you in your comfort and recovery zone?
- Which ones put you in your performance zone?
- Which make you feel panicked and overwhelmed and can put you in the panic zone?

COMFORT ZONE	PERFORMANCE ZONE	PANIC ZONE
- Sleep - Meditation - Reading - Walking in nature - Family time - Holidays	- Playing sport - Coaching - Presenting - Writing and preparing - Learning new skills - Meeting clients	- Too much work at once - Conflict - Lack of sleep - Giving feedback - Fatigue

Very often in life, we need a certain level of challenge to access our performance zone. If we are completing a task that doesn't require much concentration or intensity, we may do it sloppily.

The level of difficulty of a task is also an important component in activating our arousal zones – if a task is too easy, we stay in comfort; if it is too hard, we overtry and skills can break down.

Personality is another factor. When performing tasks in front of an audience, if you are an extrovert and are confident in completing the task, you will get energy from the anticipation.

The last factor to consider is your stage of learning. If you have certain skills that are learned and are automatic, such as passing the ball, a change in task may be required to increase your arousal levels. This can happen automatically by your opponent not giving you time or space, or by the expectation you put on yourself to hit all your passes accurately.

On the pitch

Working with some of the highest-performing teams in sport, including Tipperary, Limerick and Ballygunner, it was clear how much value each person put on balancing intensity with recovery.

The management teams planned out meticulously the scheduling of gym, pitch, team development sessions and match-day routines. The spacing between sessions enabled the players to recover properly and to spend time with their family and friends. They were not expected to be training collectively five or six times a week. They had the freedom to schedule their time outside the collective sessions. They could pursue their careers in a meaningful way, develop their relationships outside of sport and enjoy their hobbies.

What I found was that the players were fresher coming to training both mentally and physically, they were enjoying the sessions more and they were able to train and perform to higher levels on a more consistent basis. I also noticed that they picked up fewer injuries and illnesses, and that their recovery when they did was much quicker.

I have also been part of setups that believed that training harder, longer and more often was the only way to progress. I saw players lose motivation, enjoyment and appetite and, eventually, become disillusioned. Over time, their energy levels dropped, their form deteriorated and their engagement worsened. These management teams failed to value recovery, believing that taking too much time off would leave the team falling further and further behind. This drove poor behaviour in terms of overloading players and not giving them time to develop off the field, which is so important in terms of overall well-being.

It is hugely important that players look forward to team sessions. Our mood and behaviours can be dictated by the environment we create around ourselves. In my experience, if management promote positive encouragement, fun and enjoyment, rest and recovery, you see people realising their potential on a more consistent basis.

Most successful teams play the game at an intensity that other teams can't match. Barcelona FC at their best wore down opponents with the speed of their passing, and, when they lost the ball, they gave themselves five seconds to win it back. Imagine your opponent running around after the ball for two or three minutes at a time, using up valuable energy, finally winning the ball back and being swarmed and losing it again. What effect does all this chasing have on your physical and mental intensity?

Intensity is our physiological reaction to a situation. If I get a free in the last minute of the game, what effect might this have on my intensity levels? Some players would feel excited, they would see it as a great chance to win the game. They would experience a boost in positive high energy (challenged, excited) or positive low energy (calm, focused, relaxed) and would approach the situation with the expectation of success. Other players might be fearful of what could go wrong and may experience high negative energy (angry, nervous, tense) or low negative energy (lethargic, helpless, withdrawn). These different types of energy can hinder our performance in different ways. If you are too tense hitting the free, you may not have the distance on your strike. When your body is tense, it does not function effectively. If you are too relaxed, you can lack focus and become distracted more easily by opponents or by internal thoughts.

Working with players before a game is about finding – for each of them – the intensity level that will move them towards the optimal zone of performing. Players would work on this throughout the season. When warming up, what is the optimal zone they are working towards to be ready for the start of the game? What helps them to hit 4–6 on the stress/pressure scale most consistently?

Make some key considerations using the graph on page 210. Start to plot how you feel prior to training and games.

RATING PHYSICAL INTENSITY LEVELS	FEELING (NEGATIVE FEELINGS)	FEELING (POSITIVE FEELINGS)	WHAT WAS I DOING OR FOCUSING ON?
0	Inactive	Relaxed	
1	Lethargic	Content	
2	Sad	Calm	
3	Bored	Peaceful	
4	Guilty	Comfortable	
5	Nervous	Awake	
6	Tense	Alert	
7	Restless	Challenged	
8	Agitated	Excited	
9	Angry	Hyper	
10	Overwhelmed	Over-aroused	

Knowing our best intensity

We will now consider two types of intensity – positive and negative:

1. **Positive intensity** An increase in adrenaline, energy, heart rate, blood flow and muscle tension may be experienced as a positive by many competitors. Interpreting these physiological changes as positive can increase focus on the task at hand, confidence in your ability, drive to succeed, and can prepare you to meet the challenge. A high level of physiological intensity can improve the outcome of your performance, especially when it is a sport or position requiring a great deal of physical activity, such as a prop in rugby or a midfielder in hurling.

2. **Negative intensity** An increase in adrenaline, energy, heart rate, blood flow and muscle tension may be viewed as negative by less experienced competitors. When you interpret these physiological changes as negative it can affect focus – becoming too narrow (fixated on a skill that you know automatically) or too broad (taking in too much irrelevant information) – and result in poor decision-making, loss of depth perception, etc. The athlete may start to tire more quickly, have slower reactions and poorer co-ordination. They might think more negatively or feel anxious and hopeless. All these things can affect performance.

What influences our intensity levels?

1. **Perceived level of intensity** Increase in heart rate and body temperature can be interpreted by one person as 'I am warmed up and ready to go' and by another person as 'I feel very hot and I am nervous. I am not sure I am ready for this'. The person with the positive interpretation is more likely to manage the intensity successfully, whereas the person with the negative interpretation is likely to view these changes as overwhelming, which will affect performance.
2. **Task difficulty** If you are very comfortable performing a task, such as free-taking in soccer or hurling, then a lower level of intensity will be required. The lower intensity helps with focus, attention to detail, staying present and the rhythm of your skill execution. It can enable you to think more clearly and to respond with more precision. If we are involved in a fast-paced game that requires a lot of decision-making, a higher intensity is needed.

3. **Demands of the game** Most people experience lower levels of intensity in practice sessions compared to a game. One of the reasons is that expectation or outcome focus is usually not apparent when training. If you make a mistake in training, you normally won't feel as bad as when you make it during a game. There can often be less time and space in matches compared to training because players are more focused. There can be a greater desire to succeed in games than in training, as rewards are higher.

Effects of your intensity levels

1. **Over-intensity** When your intensity levels are too high, your focus might be too fixated on something or someone, for example getting revenge on someone who hit you earlier in the game, rather than moving into space to help a teammate. Your focus of attention can become too narrow, and you fail to see other cues that are relevant. You can get distracted by this focus on negative thoughts and feelings, and you can become overly focused on technique or game plan. This fearfulness and nervousness from your over-intensity can lead to muscular tension, stomach cramps/nausea, breathing issues and fatigue. These affect your performance in many ways, including reaction time, processing speed and co-ordination.
2. **Under-intensity** At times, you might have experienced levels of under-intensity, when your heart rate and energy levels were too low. You might have felt sluggish, tired and lethargic. Mentally, you might have been distracted by things in your environment,

for example supporters, the weather or opponents. Your motivation to succeed decreased.

3. **Optimal level of intensity** This is where intensity is high enough that you are focused on the task at hand, feeling energised and challenged and motivated to succeed. You are in flow, absorbed in what you're doing, with no concern for the past and not distracted by future thoughts. Through experience, you can learn how to access this optimal physical and mental intensity level that will improve your performance.

Recognising over-intensity

1. **Demands of the situation** Some games may demand more skills and qualities. If you are marking an opponent who has lots of experience, you may be over-intense in your approach. This over-trying can be detrimental to your performance. You start to force skills and decisions. You play with more tension and restriction in your movements. You play with less freedom and more fear of the outcome.
2. **Coping with the demands** The more clarity you have around the demands and the more experience you have of managing those demands, the less risk you have of being overly intense. The less confident you feel about meeting those demands, the more likely you are to be over-intense.
3. **Consequences** Identifying what failure means to you prior to a competition has an impact on intensity levels. Athletes who tell themselves 'I can't afford to lose', 'I need to win', 'I can't let others down' will affect their intensity levels to the

detriment of their performance. These are faulty assumptions that can drive over-intensity. Healthier expectations such as 'I want to win – losing would be difficult but I would learn from it' can help manage intensity levels leading into and during important competitions. Perspective is important in managing intensity levels. Sport is not life or death. Your health, career and family will still be there after the game. One game will not define your life, despite what you were told by the media or other sources.

Diving into under-intensity

1. **Complacency** If you are complacent about an event, it can be difficult to switch intensity and reach the required level for optimal performance. This lower level of intensity can impair your decision-making, movement and focus.
2. **Motivation** If you have lost interest in your sport because of a lack of form or falling out of love with the game, disagreements with players or coaches, exams or career taking precedence, then it can be difficult to have the required intensity to compete at the levels you previously hit.
3. **Overload** This can relate to having too much on your plate, for example excessive demands all at once such as six exams in two weeks, intense training sessions, issues at home with your partner or family and financial stress. These can all lead to physical and mental fatigue. You feel empty when it comes to game day and struggle to bring the required intensity to perform your role.

Mental training

We will look at ways to identify your ideal zone of performance for training and games. These will help you understand your optimum intensity for your chosen sport and how to lower or raise your intensity levels when necessary to meet a particular challenge.

Exercises

EXERCISE 1: IDEAL PERFORMANCE ZONE

Recall a prior experience where you felt you performed at your best. What were you thinking, saying, feeling and doing? What were some of the routines and actions that helped make it the best performance?

HOW DID YOU FEEL JUST BEFORE PERFORMING IN YOUR BEST GAME?		
No commitment to achieve the goal	1 2 3 4 5 6 7 8 9 10	Fully committed to achieve the goal
Low physical intensity	1 2 3 4 5 6 7 8 9 10	High physical intensity
Lack of worry	1 2 3 4 5 6 7 8 9 10	Extremely worried
Mentally calm	1 2 3 4 5 6 7 8 9 10	Mentally tense
Focused	1 2 3 4 5 6 7 8 9 10	Distracted
Low confidence	1 2 3 4 5 6 7 8 9 10	High confidence
What were you thinking or saying to yourself and focusing on just before it?		
What were you thinking or saying to yourself and focusing on during it?		
For what percentage of time do you feel you were positive, in the present moment and focused on the task at hand?		

EXERCISE 2: ADJUSTING INTENSITY LEVELS

How you approach different challenges in sport or life can result in different levels of intensity. For some challenges, a lower intensity is required, for example a closed skill, like striking a ball off a wall. Other challenges might require higher intensity, for example, tackling an opponent. Practising the skills below to increase or decrease intensity is how you reach your optimal performance zone more consistently.

INCREASING INTENSITY	DECREASING INTENSITY
- Increase speed of movement - Increase volume, speed and tone of words - Increase challenge - Use breath holds - Listen to upbeat music - Visualise intense/physical plays and behaviours - Watch intense/physical plays and behaviours - Practise embodying alertness in body language, on the toes, scanning, speaking	- Decrease speed of movements - Decrease communication to calmer and slower - Decrease challenge - Slow breaths through the nose, light and slow breathing - Listen to slow and calm music - Progressive muscle relaxation exercises - Visualise calm space and energy - Practise embodying calmness in body language, words, breathing - Ground feet and use body scan exercises

Other considerations that impact our arousal and intensity levels are:

- **Personality** If I am more of an extrovert, I may perform best when in high arousal zones. Introverted personality types may

perform best when in lower arousal zones. There are many quizzes online to figure out if you are an extrovert, introvert or even an ambivert – a mixture of the two personality types.
- **Task type** When you are performing simple skills, it is best done in high arousal, for example, tackling. Performing more complex skills, like catching a high ball coming at speed from distance, is best done in lower arousal.
- **Stage of learning** Autonomous stage (where you do not have to think about the skill you are doing) is better in higher arousal. Cognitive phase (where you must think about how to carry out the skill) is better in lower arousal.
- **Experience** Experienced athletes perform better in higher arousal zones. Novices perform better in lower arousal zones.

Reflecting on our intensity levels

Spot negative thinking patterns that contribute to your intensity level increasing or decreasing. Stop this unhelpful pattern first in training by journalling post-sessions. Recall the moments in the session when you made mistakes. What happened? What was your thought process? What were you focused on? How were you feeling? What intensity were you at during and after this mistake?

- **Practise self-talk cues** Identify the negative things you are saying to yourself in training that contribute to changes in intensity and breakdown in skills or concentration. When you become familiar with these negative thinking patterns, stop them and shift your attention back to your best focus. Self-talk is what we say to ourselves. Thoughts can come and go automatically, but we have more control over self-talk. We can build in cues that help with intensity, such as 'Be calm', 'Be smooth', 'Let go', 'Breathe and be', 'Commit to the task fully', 'Attack the ball now', 'Go fast, not rushed', 'Be here in the now'. You can find the words that resonate for you by adjusting your intensity.

- **Become familiar with the demands you will face** Watch videos of the venue you will play in. Identify the key skills you will be performing. Identify the intensity necessary to perform these skills well. Vary the intensity at which you practise. Use different opponents to test these skills. Use different times and tasks to test these skills. Study opponents and look for patterns. Identify 'what if' plans, for example if my opponent runs at me this way, then I will put my right hand into his chest to delay his momentum.
- **Power of planning** Go to the venue you will play at. Go through your routines, from when you arrive to taking the field. Simpler plans are better. These are to help you get into your zone of intensity that is optimal for you. Practise two or three routines prior to an event and be consistent with them. Practise your routines to be calm and clear in the moment, for example breathing, body language and reset thoughts: 'Next play, next task.'
- **Check in regularly** How is your physical intensity level an hour before competition? What do you want it to be at? How can you reduce it using breathing, muscle relaxation, music, social connection and play? Practise these until they are second nature

to you. If you are a novice performer, you may find it useful to be around calmer and more relaxed people. If you're an experienced performer, you may like to be around higher energy people, talking and being physically active, hitting the ball. Be around the people who encourage you and give you positive energy.

Summary

As we have seen, balancing your intensity and recovery is a critical part of high performance. Too little intensity affects your focus, where you might be easily distracted by your environment and feel unmotivated to act. With too high intensity, you feel panic and anxiety, which leads to impaired performance. It is important to understand what level of intensity works best for you. This will enable you to enter your optimal zones of recovery and performance at the right times.

Stress is an important factor in this balance, and you can learn what is positive and negative stress for you. You can learn what psychological and physiological responses your mind and body have to different stressors. How you perceive stress in important situations is a critical factor in reaching your optimal zone of performance. If we perceive the changes in our body as positive, this can harness the stress as a positive energy and enable us to meet the demands put on us.

Our perception of the demand also balances stress in our favour. If you feel you have the skills to succeed at a given task, if you focus on what specific controllable actions you can do, and if you approach success with task and behaviour goals, then you have the resources to crush the task, and this also helps with intensity/stress responses.

You are in control more than you think. You have the keys to influence your mental, emotional and physical intensity and recovery. It is a critical element of performance. Being able to identify your tendencies towards different stressors is a key awareness tool to develop. Practising how to lower or raise your intensity when you need, using the tools shared, will bring your performance to new levels. Enjoy the process of balancing the scales of intensity and recovery!

9

FRAZZLED VERSUS FLOW

ON CERTAIN DAYS, EVERYTHING SEEMS TO FLOW – effort, concentration and skills come naturally. The opposite of this flow state is feeling frazzled, when every task seems like an effort. You have competing voices in your head. Your mind is busy and loud. It is distracted and unfocused. You're hopping from past- to present- to future-based thinking. You are finding it hard to make clear decisions. Your body feels tight and tense, and you're overfocused on the mechanics of your movements and skills. It all feels like a real struggle.

Imagine playing in competition and you feel totally focused on the task at hand. Your mind is absorbed in the being and doing with no concern for anything else. It feels like things are almost happening in slow motion, but you are making split-second decisions that are enabling you to succeed. You feel in total control of your thoughts, feelings and actions. Your body feels in sync, energised and in control. Your mind is tuned into the relevant cues, and you feel a relaxed focus. You are feeling challenged by the task, but believe it is possible to overcome it.

There is excitement and enthusiasm with every move you make. There is a novelty to what you are experiencing. Your mind is particularly quiet. You are free from the usual busy, distracting thoughts and feelings and it feels like your mind, body and senses are on the one frequency working in unison. It feels blissful here. A sense of serenity comes over you. You feel like power is flowing through you and out of you.

Flow is a state of mind in which you are totally absorbed and engaged in what you are doing. You have a sense of control, you are present, you are feeling challenged but confident that your skills can meet it. You receive feedback as you go through the task. Your ego falls away, and every action, movement and thought follows inevitably from the previous one. Your whole being is involved, and you're using your skills to the utmost.

My journey to flow

In the 2010 season with Galway, I felt I truly experienced flow in my performances on a consistent basis. I had been off the panel for the previous season and had made a promise to myself that, if I did get back on the team, I would do everything in my power to be the best I could be. That season, I put a huge emphasis on my mental preparation for training and games.

I would start each week by setting very clear and specific goals. Before each training session and match, I would have routines to get me into a clear, confident and composed state of mind. For five minutes, I would mentally rehearse how I wanted to think, feel, communicate and move. I wrote out playing and training scripts of the type of person I am and wanted to be when competing. I used affirmations to help influence my mind, body and behaviours. I was priming and wiring my brain and body to be calm, composed and confident.

On waking each morning, I would start with some box-breathing techniques to calm my mind and body. I would inhale for four seconds through my nose, pause at the top of the breath for four seconds, exhale through my mouth or nose for four seconds and rest for four seconds. I would complete this for between five and ten repetitions, and it helped to regulate me into a calm and clear state in mind and body. I would practise this technique at regular intervals throughout the day and at specific moments like when I arrived at a venue, after the warm-up, after the parade, halfway through each half, half-time and the last five minutes of each half.

Other activities I liked to do each morning and on arrival at the venue were light movements to see how the body felt. Was it tight or loose, tense or relaxed? I would start to wake up and activate my body through gentle stretches and dynamic movements to feel alert and lively. I would check in to see what intensity I was at and increase or lower my arousal levels based on that feeling. I would release any pent-up anxiety or nervous energy by striking a fast ball off a wall and tuning into the feel of the ball and the strike. I would count my strikes and engage my brain. I would check my gear one last time before the team huddle. I would then go out on the field with the team and engage in our warm-up routine.

During the warm-up routine on the field, I would engage in box breathing at different times to remain calm, clear and composed. I would check if my body language was strong and confident with my head up, eyes on my target, chest out. I would connect with my teammates and the task we were doing, with no concern for the past or predictions for the future. I would challenge myself to focus in the moment, execute one ball at a time and aim to get my execution right.

Before the start of the game, I would check the positioning on the field of my backs, midfielders and forwards. I would remind myself through verbal cues to be in the moment. I used the word *'vamos'* ('let's go' in Spanish) anytime I found my mind drifting from present-moment awareness.

I set myself challenges, such as winning the ball anytime it came into my area. If I saw a teammate in possession, I would make smart runs to support him. If I was on the ball, I was going to give it to my teammates. If my man gained possession, I would put him under ferocious pressure and aim to dispossess him or force him into a poor decision. I would communicate positively and consistently with myself. I would let mistakes go and get back to the next ball as fast as possible.

I found that taking the game in short fifteen- to thirty-second bursts, with clear points to focus on and short reminders, kept me composed, focused in the present and confident. The recovery strategies after each sequence were the same: three to five rounds of box breathing to be composed, clear and present, check shoulders and head up to feel confident, communicate next task, *vamos* or connect with teammates.

Breaking the game down into one-minute blocks helped me focus deeply and concentrate on what was important now to help the team to succeed in that moment. There was a challenge every ten to fifteen seconds and I began to love these small wins in front of me. I tried to collect as many as I could in each one-minute block.

One flow experience that stood out that season was the Tipperary All-Ireland quarter-final. There were periods in the second half when high balls were raining down on our half-back line. I had rehearsed these moments so often, seeing the ball coming and me exploding off the ground and catching it at its highest point. I was just arriving at the flight of the ball with perfect timing with no concern for what might happen. Total absorption and engagement in the challenge in front of me. It felt like time slowed down as I hung in the air making these catches and coming to ground evading tackles and finding my teammates with possession. I felt so alive at that moment. My mind and body were alert, in control and in sync. It felt effortless, as if I was having an out-of-body experience.

That season was one of my most consistent in a Galway jersey. From not being on the panel the previous season, I went from fourth-choice centre-back to first choice. I started every game bar one league game. We won the Walsh Cup and National League and lost the All-Ireland quarter-final to Tipperary by a point. I was nominated for an All-Star award and was asked to be vice-captain of the team at the end of the year. I felt my playing stats hit new levels in terms of possessions, positive decision-making, tackles and score creation.

Above all, I felt completely energised in games. My mind was so focused on the present that negativity and distraction seemed to dissolve from my thought patterns. I felt my mind and body were in total sync in most games. I played with great freedom and loved the sense of clarity, ease and flow to my game.

Feeling frazzled

Have you been in situations in life where you did not feel in flow? When your mind was feeling frazzled. When you were overthinking skills that were usually automatic to you. When you were second-guessing your every move. When you were picking up on lots of negative chatter in your head and were finding it hard to focus on any one thing. When you were worrying frequently about not messing up. When you were picking up irrelevant information that was hindering your performance, such as the opposition manager, people in the crowd, what people might be thinking of you.

It is not easy to perform at your best when your mind is in this frazzled state. It is not easy to move with ease when you're feeling tense, panicked and overwhelmed. It is not easy to execute the important skills when you are experiencing these negative internal or external distractions.

The good news is that you can learn to prime your mind and body before these situations to move from frazzled to focused. You can learn to manage your thoughts, feelings and behaviours. You can learn to feel in control and confident in these situations.

The following are the factors that help with accessing your flow.

1. **Identify an activity, you are deeply passionate about and interested in.** It could be sports, career, music, etc. Taking the example of sport, begin to identify the areas of your sport that you are most interested in. Are there skills you prefer doing? Do you execute these best in isolation or in small groups? Do you feel full absorption working one-v-one with or against a teammate? What makes it challenging and rewarding for you?
2. **When you are doing this activity, how does it make you feel?** When you are in flow, your brain releases five powerful chemicals that influence learning, motivation, creativity and performance, namely norepinephrine, dopamine, endorphins, anandamide and serotonin.
    - Norepinephrine and dopamine strengthen focus, helping you to block out distractions. You can recognise emerging patterns of play more quickly and can produce creative solutions.
    - Endorphins block pain, letting you push through fatigue or tiredness.
    - Anandamide prompts lateral connections and generates insights greater than most brainstorming sessions.
    - Serotonin, that feel-good chemical, bonds teammates together, helping you be in sync with your team and go the extra yards for each other.

The only time these five chemicals are in unison is during flow. It makes activities like sport more pleasurable, meaningful and addictive. Can you think of specific instances when some or all of these big five chemicals were at play?

3. **What strengths are you using while doing this activity?** These might be your focus, your anticipation, your intensity. Are there certain skills that you are completely confident and at ease using in many different scenarios? What are they? What challenges do you use them for most consistently? Where do these strengths give you an advantage? You could be extremely good at scanning in crowded areas for teammates and very accurate at passing into tight areas, for example.

4. **How challenging do you feel the activity is?** Are you in total control of your skills or just on the edge of stretching yourself? One of the psychological triggers is the challenge/skills ratio. Your attention is most engaged when there's a very specific relationship between the difficulty of a task and your ability to perform that task. If your challenge is too high, for example above your current skills by more than 4 per cent, then your fear response overrides your mind and body system. If the challenge is too easy, you stop paying attention and become distracted. Flow appears near the emotional midpoint between boredom and anxiety. This flow channel is where the task is hard enough to make you stretch, but not hard enough to make you become panicked or overwhelmed.

5. **What feedback do you receive while doing it?** How do you correct yourself during the task? When performing tasks in sport

you are solving multiple problems in rapid time. Mistakes can happen given the speed of your decision-making. How do you respond to these mini mistakes? Do you quickly find another way to solve the task at hand? For example, you are running past an opposition player and he attempts to block your run. You see him coming towards you and so you evade him by changing direction.

Activate your flow state

It is important to look at what will get you into your flow state more consistently. Flow is defined as an optimal state of being awake and aware of your surroundings, where you feel your best and perform at your best. You experience moments of complete attention and total absorption when you become so focused on the task at hand that everything else disappears. Action and awareness merge as one. Your sense of self disappears (your 'inner worrier' is quiet). Your sense of time can slow down or speed up. Your mental and physical performance goes to new levels.

The present moment can feel effortless. There is an internal joy to what you're doing. It is intrinsically rewarding just doing the task; you do not seek or need outside validation. You feel a powerful sense of control over the situation, that your skills are stretched but can meet the challenge. You might have a sense of struggle at the beginning before you release your skills, struggles dissolve and you enter a serene state.

How can you trigger your flow state?

Flow can only arise when all your attention is focused on the present moment. Psychologist Mihaly Csikszentmihalyi, who researched the secrets to happiness, found that flow state was an important factor. He describes eight characteristics of flow:

1. Complete concentration on the task.
2. Clarity of goals and reward in mind and immediate feedback.
3. Transformation of time (speeding up/slowing down).
4. The experience is intrinsically rewarding.
5. Effortlessness and ease.
6. There is a balance between challenge and skills.
7. Actions and awareness are merged, losing self-conscious rumination.
8. There is a feeling of control over the task.

Can you reflect on experiences you have had in the past few weeks in which all these conditions were met?

On the pitch

In 2021, working with Ballygunner, we faced an extremely difficult task in that year's Munster final. The mental challenge for many of the players was to not allow stories of past Munster final defeats cloud their perception and judgement of the present moment. To overcome this challenge, we needed to ensure that all the players had upgraded their subconscious programmes towards approaching success rather than avoiding failure.

To avoid becoming frazzled by the memories of the past, we worked very specifically on our focus being on this challenge only. Those past defeats had happened to some members of our panel, but this was a new team, with new qualities, new goals and a new mentality to deal with distractions better.

We had a very clear mission: to be the first team from the club to win an All-Ireland.

We had a very clear identity of who we were and how we wanted to live this in representing our team, club and community. We had a very clear process of how we were going to play together, and we shared the responsibility of success across the whole group. Everyone's role was important, and we would help and care for each other on the journey. We all contributed; we all brought qualities and skills that added to the group in a variety of ways. Everyone's voice mattered, and we realised the impact of our words and behaviours on others.

It was wonderful to see the team in flow in that Munster final performance. We took control of every position and line on the field. Players were in control of their minds and bodies. They were regularly communicating with each other verbally and non-verbally. They were in sync in terms of their movements on and off the ball. They moved effortlessly between defence and attack. They transitioned quickly into the right positions on their own and opposition puckouts. They moved the ball with intelligence, both short and long, to the man in the best position. They made the right decisions often, in and out of possession. It felt like there was an energy and momentum, and you could sense the connection, understanding and trust within the group.

Mental training

The states you identify will impact your ability to access flow. It is important that you reflect on your own experiences to identify what states were present as you completed certain tasks.

One of the important factors in flow is balancing the level of challenge with your current skills. If the challenge is too big and your skills are not adequate, you may feel anxiety or worry. If the challenge is too small, boredom and apathy might set in.

Think of the things you enjoy doing, be it meeting friends, playing a sport or the creative aspects of your career. How do you feel while doing these things? There might be a sense of joy, excitement, challenge, happiness, etc.

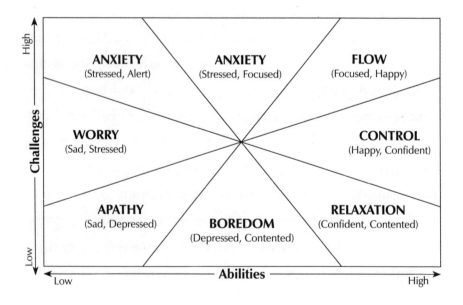

Using the graph on the previous page, you can start to look at the different challenges you have on and off the field and match these high/low challenges to how you feel and what level of ability/skill they take to execute them.

1. Identify in each area which activities put you into a state of boredom (e.g. watching soaps), worry (e.g. thinking about war) or relaxation (e.g. being in nature, walking or sea swimming). Think also, in the context of your sport, which skills put you into arousal, at the edge of your comfort zone (e.g. tackling one-v-one, finding a pass in a two-v-one situation, dealing with aerial balls). Which activities put you into a state of control (e.g. shooting from forty yards out on the run, getting a handpass on the run or taking a free close in)?
2. Which activities do you do each day (outside sport) that lead to experiences of arousal – the feeling that you have just passed the edge of your comfort zone and are learning something new? It is an important condition for flow to occur. But if it's too high, you can feel anxious; too low, and you can become bored. You might be working on a skill at 100 per cent speed and it is breaking down all the time on you. To regain control, you might need to bring it down to 90 per cent.
3. Which activities do you do each day that lead to feelings of control? You might feel very comfortable doing them, but they might not be challenging enough for you to access flow. It may be necessary for you to increase the challenge, for example marking a more physical or faster opponent in sport or writing

a thousand words for your new book. It could be creating a new dummy to evade opponents in sport.

Aim to stretch and challenge yourself in the control zone every day and see how you feel. Identify your arousal activities, where that balance of skill and challenge meets. Notice how you feel and how you regulate emotions when struggle and stretch is happening. This is a great time to use your mental-skills practices, like breathwork, self-talk and attention control.

What else must we consider in flow states?

Traditionally it was held that we use only 10 per cent of our brains. However, research on flow suggests that this is not the case. Flow utilises the brain powerfully, and it has been shown in the work by Steven Kotler from the Flow Research Collective that flow is a major factor in science breakthroughs, gold medals in sport, etc., while top executives in business are two to five times more productive in flow states than those out of flow.

What happens to our brain when we are in flow? We shut down the prefrontal cortex, which means we no longer separate the past, present or future. Our sense of self and time dissolves. We become one with the task. Our whole being is absorbed in the doing. We are hacking our brain chemistry.

In addition to the characteristics of flow described earlier by Csikszentmihalyi (see page 236), Steven Kotler (2014) identified four additional triggers:

1. High consequences (there is some element of risk, be it physical, mental or emotional).
2. Deep embodiment (it is a multi-sensory experience – uses all your five senses; you are learning through doing).
3. Environment (it is unpredictable, complex and with lots of novelty).
4. Creativity (linking ideas together and recognising patterns).

Exercise

YOUR TASK FOR NOW

1. Identify a sporting activity that you are interested in and passionate about, for example GAA, soccer or rugby.
2. Identify your core strengths, such as catching a high ball, accurate passing, making smart runs to support teammates.
3. Set a challenge that is on the limits of your potential. You are deeply engaged in it but not overwhelmed by it.
4. Set clear and specific goals around that task or challenge. Set your outcome goals, such as making five clean catches in your next game/training, to complete 90 per cent accurate passes, to make five clear support runs in each half. Set your process goals that help achieve this: attack and catch, head up, scan and pass, and move to support your teammate.
5. Identify what your best intensity and focus levels are for this task (see Chapter 8).

6. List any potential distractions and how you might deal with them, for example: 'If I make a mistake then I will respond by employing my reset routine using breathing, body language and self-talk cues.'
7. Have regular and immediate feedback, for example: 'Did I attack and catch it? Did I get my head up, scan and pass? Did I make a smart support run or not?'
8. Focus on the process-related actions each time. This helps us to stay present and not become overwhelmed with the challenge or too much information at once. Make sure you have set action-related goals to help you achieve five clean catches, for example: 'I will position myself just behind my man on a high ball. I will time my run and jump. I will use my hurl to protect the space. I will catch with my fingers at the highest point.'
You could simplify this to cue words such as 'position, attack, clear and catch'. Having these short cues will ensure you do not overload your short-term memory. It will help you to immerse yourself in the doing. You know these skills. Performing is not the time to be going through the mechanics of the skill or focusing on the outcomes. Just engage fully in the actions of the skill.

Summary

Flow is not unique to high performers in sport, business or entertainment. It is something you can learn to access by setting the right conditions. It is a feeling of deep focus on what you are doing and clear objectives around what you are trying to achieve, be it to execute a skill in sport, business or education. Your awareness and attention are submerged in the doing. There is an intensity and intent to what you are doing. Your skills are challenged and stretched but you feel in control. You know what you are doing at each moment. Time flies by or slows down. You become one with the activity.

You can access flow on a consistent basis. You can set the conditions for it to occur. You can identify what activity you care about, have a passion for and a deep interest in. You can set clear and specific goals to meet any challenge you want to overcome.

You can identify the mental states that help with accessing flow by being on the edge of arousal (stretched but not overwhelmed) or by being in control without being too comfortable. You can focus with the right intent by having clear moment-to-moment actions. These clear and specific actions will enable your brain to reduce irrelevant distractions. You can correct as you move through the task-related actions with immediate feedback.

You can begin to lose your sense of self and time through this total absorption and immersion in the task at hand. You can be at one with the task with no concerns or distractions. You can enjoy this feeling where just being in the activity is reward. You can feel a sense of ecstasy and serenity even in the most perceived pressure environments by influencing the main factors we have discussed.

10

RESISTANCE VERSUS ACCEPTANCE

WHEN YOU ARE APPROACHING SITUATIONS THAT matter to you, it is natural to experience anxiety, worry and doubt. Your brain has been designed to scan for threats, to look for the negative. To protect you and keep you safe, it searches for threats most of your waking hours.

These threats can be physical, mental or emotional. When faced with a situation where the result is unpredictable, we may feel discomfort mentally: 'Will I be able to do this?' We might feel anxious and experience chest tightening, shallow breathing and body temperature changes.

So, what can we do in such situations?

There is an approach called *acceptance*. Acceptance is our acknowledgement of the reality of a situation without attempting to change it or fight it. Sport is absolutely going to be tough and challenging, both mentally and physically. There will be times when we might feel like giving in.

Acceptance can be used to build mental flexibility when approaching situations. You make sense of experiences through your thoughts, feelings, sensations and behaviours. Acceptance enables you to recognise and accept uncomfortable thoughts and feelings, while taking committed action towards what you value. Through a better understanding of the relationship between your thoughts, feelings, sensations and behaviours, you can better understand yourself, as well as your environment, enabling you to take the action necessary to move you towards your values, aspirations and goals.

Acceptance can help you build mental flexibility and develop both resilience and a growth mindset, to stay focused on your goals, face challenges and learn to cope with the setbacks that can occur in sport. By understanding how to better manage your thoughts, feelings and behaviours, you can become more self-aware and increase your level of performance.

The main goal of acceptance is to help you recognise your thoughts and feelings, accept them, and then make changes to move towards your goals. The process requires you to allow for unpleasant feelings that come up without letting these feelings negatively affect your performance. For example, if you're feeling anxious before an important game, you can acknowledge that anxiety as part of your performance – validate it as normal – and then choose to focus on the key tasks you need to perform in the match. This mental approach is beneficial because it helps you develop a more resilient attitude towards your sporting performance. It encourages you to take ownership of your values, and to commit to the goals and actions that are meaningful to you. This involves focusing on personal development rather than the outcome of events or competitions.

The opposite of acceptance is *resistance*. To sidestep or get rid of uncomfortable thoughts and feelings, such as nerves or anxiety, you might avoid training or avoid a conversation with your coach about your performance. These may give you temporary respite in the moment but will heighten your anxiety the next time the situation appears. You have a choice to make at this point: move away from your values (identified in Chapter 1) or move towards your values with committed action. One of these choices brings growth; the other brings frustration and despair.

My journey to acceptance

In 2013, I had a very difficult time on and off the field. At the beginning of the season, I was struggling for form and fitness in training and finding it very hard to motivate myself. I felt flat, lethargic and drained. Having played most of the Walsh Cup, league and championship in 2012, and having been nominated for an All-Star, to not feature at all in 2013 was a very difficult experience for me.

I didn't start any of the pre-season, league or Leinster championship games. I felt I was drifting further back in the pecking order. I was not seeing any hope in terms of selection or game time. Week by week different players were being tried in the centre-back position; by the end of the league, six different players had been tried with varying degrees of success. This was frustrating me more and more because I knew I wasn't hitting the levels I was capable of in training to warrant more opportunities.

For several weeks, I got no feedback from management on what my role was or what I had to do to improve my form. I also resisted having that conversation with them out of fear of hearing that I was surplus to requirements. These were some of the assumptions my mind was coming up with. I was feeling angry, frustrated and disappointed with the lack of communication and direction. I was not accepting that this was the reality of my situation. I didn't realise it at the time, but this resistance was impacting my way forward.

My resistance to speaking with management was holding me back. My resistance to my new role of trying to get back on the team was holding me back from improving. My resistance to not being given more opportunities to play, the belief that I deserved more, was holding me back from embracing this new challenge and enjoying the journey of improving. I was in a negative, outcome-focused mindset during this period.

After the league, I knew I had to do something different. It was time to accept that my position in the squad was fighting to make the team and that my form was not up to the level required. I decided I needed to speak with management to let them know how

I was feeling and to look for guidance. I asked them to meet with me after a Saturday-morning session. We sat down in the dressing room. I was feeling very uncomfortable and anxious before it. I could feel my body temperature soaring. I felt my face becoming flushed.

I wanted to find a solution. I wanted to get my form back as quickly as possible. I wanted to be in contention for a place on the team. I told them how I had felt over the past few months. That as the only player from last year's side not to see any game time, I felt that I was being made a scapegoat for the All-Ireland final defeat. I was close to tears. I asked them why they had looked at everyone bar me for the centre-back position, despite my excellent form over the past three years.

These things were challenging to admit to myself and to express to management. But when I'd said them, I saw how negative my outlook had been. I knew I was feeling angry, frustrated and disappointed, but I hadn't shared those feelings with anyone or really accepted why. When it all came out, I could feel the resistance lifting from my shoulders and chest.

In fairness to management, they listened. They said they recognised how I was feeling and told me that I was an important member of the group and that if I came to training with an improved attitude, focus and effort, and found my form, I would be in contention for the next championship game, which was the All-Ireland quarter-final against Clare.

Looking back, I had not accepted the discomfort of my situation. I had failed to notice the negative impact my thoughts, feelings and behaviours were having on my mindset. I was resisting the fact that my form was not good enough, that I was not as mentally focused on the process as I needed to be. That I was bringing a negative attitude and approach.

I was too focused on myself and resisting what was being fed back to me. I was resisting that this was a new season, and that management had to base selection on attitude, effort and form.

In the days following the meeting, I began to feel like a heavy weight had been lifted from me, one that I had been carrying for six months. I began to enjoy training much more and got back to a decent level of form. By quarter-final time, I had put myself back in the selection picture. My perspective was validated when management came to me in training and told me I was back in good form, and I was in with a chance to come on. I told them I was ready and would help the team in any way I could. Unfortunately, defeat to Clare knocked us out of the championship, and I didn't get the opportunity to help the team on the field that day.

On the bus home, I had a sinking feeling that this could be the end of my journey with Galway at twenty-nine years of age. I had played one competitive game all year, in the Railway Cup. I knew the manager had probably lost faith in me and didn't value my contribution anymore.

Over the course of the summer, a lot of the management team were let go. It was unexpected, given that, the previous year, we had won the county's first Leinster title and got to an All-Ireland final. Was there a need to lose our main coach, doctor, strength and conditioning coach and physical therapist from our backroom team?

I got the call that I was surplus to requirements too. My intuition had been right that day on the bus home. My senior career had been cut short for a second time. This time felt different, though, as I didn't see any way back with the manager staying on for two more seasons.

It took me a couple of years to come to terms with my career ending in this way. I felt very bitter towards the management for how I had been treated. I had devoted a huge amount of effort and time and had sacrificed so many things to be a county hurler from the age of thirteen. I found it hard to accept that I couldn't fulfil my dream of winning an All-Ireland senior title for my county. I felt I had a huge amount to offer in terms of leadership, competition for places and helping to develop standards within the group environment. It took time to accept what had happened and to start focusing on my new reality.

Feeling resistant

Have you had moments in your life where you felt resistant to what was happening? Wanting things to go back to how they were, thinking that if people hadn't made certain decisions and just left everything the way it was, you would be fine. Sometimes, life does not go in the direction you expect or would like it to go.

This can be hard to deal with if you put a barrier up and don't accept that the change has happened.

You can begin to experience a host of confusing feelings. You might be in denial about what happened. You might feel anger towards that person or situation. You might go into bargaining mode where you make promises to yourself or others that, if it happens again, you will do things differently. You might feel hopeless and depressed by it. You feel a level of sadness and longing for that relationship, person or situation.

These are all very natural, normal feelings to have as you move through your resistance to what is happening. As you process the situation, these feelings will occur at different stages. The important thing to be aware of is what stage you are at. Is it denial, anger, bargaining or sadness?

When you begin to process the sadness of the situation and what has happened, you are almost ready to move to acceptance. This is when you find that the intensity of the sadness has lessened somewhat. You can accept what has happened and that you can enjoy the sport or pastime in a new way. Dealing with the feelings the change has brought up will have been a struggle, but it is through these struggles that our greatest growth in character can happen. Life is a great teacher if you are open to the learnings in each experience.

Choose to accept

Unfortunately, at times, we suffer pain, change and loss – losing games, losing a loved one through illness or losing a job. Change is an inevitable part of being human. How we process change is different for everyone. I have found the Kübler-Ross model (2014) to be beneficial in this regard. It helps us to understand where we are at mentally within the change process.

Think of a change you are going through or might encounter shortly in your sport or personal life. Try to identify the stage you are currently at using the adapted Kübler-Ross graph below. Try to identify the steps you can take to move to your next phase of growth.

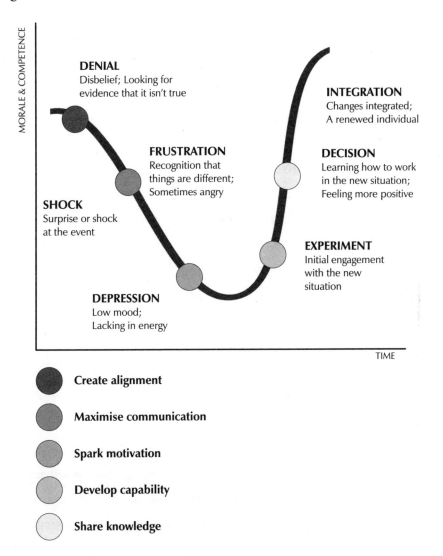

Initially, you might be hit with a decision that surprises you. You are dropped from the team or panel. You feel surprise and shock at the decision. This is stage one for you. It is important to communicate the change to those closest to you, without too much depth at first.

The next stage is denial. You do not believe the change is going to happen or that it is going to impact you. It is important to communicate who told you about the change, what it is, when it is happening and why it is happening. You might go into denial that it ever happened or think this is just a bad dream. How could this be? What is the reason I was dropped?

The next stage is frustration. You feel a decrease in effort and productivity. You are questioning and pushing back against this change. You want to hold on to the way things were. You feel a sense of disbelief and look for evidence that it is not true. You then start to move to a feeling of frustration. You recognise that things are different, and it brings up moments of anger and frustration for you. It has happened, and when you think about it you are angry about the decision.

The next stage is depression. You recognise the change is happening. It is inevitable and you feel a sense of loss for the way things were. It must happen, things will be different. Your motivation and productivity are at their lowest here. You are in a low mood, lacking motivation and energy for life. You lack interest in everyday life, be it work, relationships or sport. It is important now that you reach out to people who are ahead of this stage to support you.

Next is the experimental stage. You are recognising the change and learning more about how it will impact you day-to-day. You begin to identify the things you can and want to focus on. There is quite a bit of excitement now about the potential of the change. You experiment with different choices available to you. Some of these might be helpful, such as a new exercise routine, meeting new people or trying new things.

In the decision stage, you come to an acceptance of sorts about the new way of thinking and doing. You begin to make decisions that move you forward. You begin to share knowledge about what you have learned from your experiences and journey so far. You look at how you can use these experiences in a meaningful way in the present and future.

In the final stage – integration – you begin to incorporate the changes into your daily routines, such as spending more time with family or friends, and you look at opportunities in other areas of life. You have more time to train by yourself and improve aspects you are weak on. You have more time for the club and find enjoyment and form again.

The change will enable you to focus on your career a bit more. You can travel. You can start a course you might have put off. You begin to feel more positive.

You see the benefits this new situation will have for your mental health, relationships and career. You start to integrate these new routines and changes into your life and feel optimistic about the present and the future.

Acceptance and Commitment Therapy

The other tool that is extremely helpful when facing challenging situations is Acceptance and Commitment Therapy, and particularly the model called Hexaflex for developing psychological flexibility.

Acceptance and Commitment Therapy (ACT) is a third-wave Cognitive-Behavioural Therapy (CBT), centred on the idea of acceptance, presence and values-focused life as an approach to managing mental-health challenges. ACT assumes the idea that the human brain is an outdated machine that, sooner or later, will cause psychological distress for everyone. As such, it is assumed that the brain will inevitably cause pain. With this in consideration, ACT aims for people to live a meaningful and values-oriented life, while learning to accept the pain that unavoidably comes with it. Rather than see the pain in life as something to avoid at all costs, it teaches us to view it as the price of admission for a rich life.

Psychological flexibility is defined as being in contact with the present moment, fully aware of emotions, sensations and thoughts, welcoming them, including the undesired ones, and moving in a pattern of behaviour in the service of your chosen values. To be accepting of your own thoughts and emotions and acting on your long-term values rather than short-term impulses, thoughts and feelings that are often linked to experiential avoidance and a way to control unwanted inner events.

It is a psychological framework that enables you to take a mindful approach to dealing with challenging thoughts, feelings and behaviours. It helps you to become more open, flexible and adaptable to your experience while also taking committed action towards your values and goals. The matrix consists of six interrelated processes: acceptance, cognitive defusion, meeting the present moment, self-context, values and committed action.

The first area is *values*, and these represent your guiding principles and standards of behaviour. They also represent your beliefs about what you feel to be right and just in the world. They clarify your strengths when you act on them and can bring purpose and meaning to what you do in life. Clarifying your values and living by them helps you to stay on track and make decisions about what matters in your life. For example, you might value being good at sport. You make choices each day to become better at your sport. You might value being honest in life. You demonstrate honesty through your sport by putting strong effort into practice and preparation. You might show it in matches by competing hard for every ball. You might show it by getting back quickly when the team loses possession. These values guide your decisions when they become clear and intentional in this way.

The next area focuses on *committed action*. It is the process of making a conscious and meaningful choice to engage in behaviours that align with your values and goals, even if these behaviours cause temporary discomfort, worry or fear. Committed action includes planning, goal-setting and taking steps towards important behaviours, dealing with obstacles and accepting yourself unconditionally for your efforts, no matter the outcome.

The next stage is *self-context*. This is about recognising that you are much more than just your thoughts. Sometimes, you can get caught up in identifying who you are with what you think. 'I am not a confident person' might be one such thought that can impact all parts of your life. You start to accept this as true and pull back or avoid situations for fear of not being up to the task. It is important to be aware of your thoughts and to challenge the truth of them when it is affecting your fulfilment in life.

Acceptance is another stage of the matrix. It requires you to be open to and accepting of your thoughts, feelings, emotions and physical sensations, without judgement or evaluation. This enables you to move away from a focus on what is unacceptable, enabling you to accept life as it is happening for you right now. Acceptance does not mean 'giving in' or 'agreeing with' what you are feeling or experiencing, but rather being open to whatever discomfort or difficulty you may be facing in the present moment. You might be feeling angry about a decision by your teammate or referee. You accept your anger in relation to their decisions or behaviour and acknowledge why you are angry. This does not mean you give in or agree with the feeling; it just means you have acknowledged it, and it is not holding power over you. It gives you the mental space to respond from your values rather than react from this angry feeling.

The next skill is called *cognitive defusion*, the process of distancing yourself from your thoughts and beliefs. Your thoughts are not always true and not always false. They are just thoughts. Recognising that thoughts are merely patterns of words and images in your mind helps you to move away from the automatic associations you might have with them. You can then choose to reframe your thoughts and observe them in a more objective way, thus reducing the unhelpful influence they have on your behaviour. Just because your mind generates a thought that you can't beat an opponent does not make it 100 per cent true. Cognitive defusion enables you to observe the thought without hooking onto it. It gives you the mental space to separate yourself from the thought.

The next skill, *meeting the present moment*, involves noticing, observing and engaging with whatever is happening in your environment. This may include physical sensations, emotions and thoughts. It encourages you to become aware of your internal and external experiences without getting caught up in those experiences. Engaging in the present moment enables you to gain perspective on the entire situation and take mindful action. You can use your five senses to bring your awareness back to the present moment. You can observe your thoughts without engaging in them; you can listen for sounds; you can feel your breath going in and out your nose; you can taste; you can smell; you can be aware of touch, be it your feet on the ground, breeze on your face or squeezing your wrist.

The next key skill is *mindfulness*, part of *meeting the present moment*, is being aware and present in the moment. Being the observer of your thoughts, feelings or sensations. It involves letting go of past stories, judgements and expectations, and being mindful of your thoughts, feelings and sensations of the present moment. Practising mindfulness can help you to increase your emotional stability, intelligence and flexibility, thereby enabling you to better respond to difficult and challenging situations.

Overall, the Acceptance Commitment Therapy Hexaflex matrix helps you to take an open and mindful approach to life's challenges. It can help you to engage in behaviours that are congruent with your values and goals. It encourages you to accept and be open to your everyday experiences and requires you to engage with the present moment more consistently. It also helps you to develop the self-awareness of observing your thoughts and beliefs and to act in a meaningful way.

On the pitch

In 2022, I started working with an inter-county hurler and All-Ireland winner. We looked at creating more mental flexibility in his approach to games. He was spending a lot of time in the lead-up to games worrying about what others might be saying about his performances, and then, after games, looking for outside validation on social media.

We started by looking at his values in sport. What behaviours would make his family proud on the field? What behaviours would he like his teammates to see in him? For him, courage was the most important moral value, and so we broke down what this would look like on and off the ball.

He defined key behaviours, such as attacking the ball, committing to finding teammates with accurate strikes and being vocal to help organise the defence. We looked at other values, such as health, family, partner, friends and career, and identified opportunities where he could live consistently and in line with his values on a moment-by-moment and day-to-day basis. He began to see life as a canvas on which he could express courage each day as a son, partner or leader in his team. He could live authentically in each moment by moving towards his values. He felt greater purpose and meaning in every interaction and lived in alignment with his courage value.

Over the course of the season, we identified areas where he was not feeling fulfilled. An issue he had with one of the coaches was something that needed to be addressed. He outlined his thoughts, feelings, sensations and how he behaved around this coach, and it became clear that he showed a lack of confidence when in the coach's presence. He believed that as the coach had won an All-Ireland, his opinion and ideas were 'always right'. This belief held him back from expressing his true feelings – he had huge respect for the coach's achievements and was consequently neglecting the fact he himself had as much to offer.

He was moving away from his own values of speaking with courage, and his approach on the field also became inhibited at times by worrying about making mistakes in front of the coach.

We identified some things that he could control and change. We looked at what he could accept was outside of his control and how it was making him feel. We looked at how he could give himself some mental space from feelings of anger and frustration. He used present-moment awareness tools, like box breathing, body scans and centring techniques. These enabled him not to be hijacked by the negative thoughts and feelings being generated by his experiences. He realised he couldn't change some of his coach's traits but could change his reactions to them. This was empowering for him, and he began to focus on his own strengths again.

Having clarity around his values and key principles of behaviour was fantastic for him. When he faced new and challenging situations, he would constantly refer to the most courageous version of himself and how that person would react. This enabled him to move towards his values and goals on a more consistent basis. We identified key goals for him using process, performance and outcome goals (see Chapter 3). We identified clear plans for how he could measure and rate his preparation, training and performances.

This is what his plan and goals looked like.

PERSON I AM – COURAGEOUS AND HARD-WORKING	HARD-WORKING PREPARATIONS	COURAGEOUS AND HARD-WORKING – PROCESS IN GAME

• Courageous by:
  • Speaking my truths
  • Playing life on the front foot by taking risks
• Hard-working through effort and being prepared and ready
	• Sleep eight hours
	• Mindful breathing practice
	• Visualisation
	• Nutrition
	• Recovery routines
	• Gym goals
	• Deliberate practice goals
		• Communicate positive body language and task-specific words
		• Attack the ball
		• Commit to my strikes
		• Reset between plays quickly

It was also important to identify patterns of thinking, feeling and behaving when he felt he was not living with courage. We identified some situations on and off the field when his behaviours were not moving him towards his values of being courageous and consistent at his sport. This helped him to spot these unhelpful patterns more quickly. He was then able to self-correct through accepting what he was feeling and behaving more courageously in those moments by putting in greater effort, demanding the ball or speaking his truths around what he was observing.

Mental training

Which are the most beneficial pillars of ACT that you can bring into practice daily? Which pillar would provide the most benefits to your life right now?

Committing to living a values-based life takes effort but the rewards are huge. It is normal to experience anxiety at times – the important skill is to accept this rather than avoiding the anxiety or trying to get rid of it. Acceptance can help you move towards the person you want to be and the goals you want to achieve.

Firstly, identify what values are most important to you in sport. Is it to be determined? Committed? Relentless? Then write down some of the behaviours that show that relentlessness on and off the ball. Write down some of the behaviours that show that relentlessness off the field.

Secondly, identify some of the behaviours that take you away from being relentless on and off the ball and off field. It is good to capture some of these avoidance behaviours that are not serving you. These might be behaviours like not demanding the ball after a mistake for fear of making another mistake. They could be behaviours like not communicating to teammates when going through a poor period in a game.

Thirdly, in a previous experience when you were engaged in these avoidance behaviours, what were you thinking prior to them? Were these thoughts helpful? Did they make you feel better? If the answer is no, then it is time to change.

You can change by taking a pause and choosing an approach behaviour. You can focus your attention on the present moment using breath, listening for sounds or feeling your feet on the ground. You can notice positive thoughts and go with them instead. You can create pauses between thoughts that enable you to take a different course for your train of thought.

At different times, you might notice different trains of thought. These might carry negative and unhelpful thoughts. They might carry neutral thoughts that have neither a positive nor negative effect on your feelings and behaviours. They might carry positive and helpful thoughts that provide positive feelings and behaviours for you. You can learn to recognise these positive, neutral and negative thoughts.

Mindfulness is a great way to become more aware of your thoughts, feelings, sensations and behaviours. You can better identify through mindful awareness what plane you are currently on, and through cognitive defusion, you can learn not to get caught up or attached to thoughts, be they positive, negative or neutral. Sometimes, when you are anxious or worried, you might get hooked onto the thought 'I can't handle this', and this will lead to feeling scared, worried and tense. With practice you can learn to let this thought fly away.

You do not have to change every negative thought you have to a positive one. You do not have to let thoughts decide your behaviour. You have the choice to defuse from your thoughts and behave in a way that makes you fulfilled.

Summary

You are on this planet to live a fulfilled life. Part of living is facing challenges and overcoming experiences that are not easy. The best moments in life can come when you are stretched mentally, physically and emotionally. Your efforts are stretched voluntarily to experience something worthwhile.

You feel anxious, scared and worried. These are normal human feelings to have when you are faced with challenges. How often in your life have you felt excited, nervous or anxious when doing something that was passive or unchallenging? How have you felt when succeeding at something that was slightly above your perceived capabilities? The point here is that anxiety, nerves or excitement are not dissimilar feelings. Your body and mind are alert, alive and awake. You know something is about to happen. You haven't got full control over the outcome but you're here and ready to go. You might not know it yet, but this could be the most exciting thing you do in your life. It could be one of your greatest achievements.

When you take risks, there are rewards too. It could be the feeling of exhilaration and joy at having surpassed your own expectations. These can be the best moments in life when, in your head, you had stacked the odds against yourself. Despite the uncomfortable feelings, you moved forward towards your dream. You took value-based actions that enabled you to not resist but embrace what is most valued to you. That is success, that is living life. That is fulfilment.

The key things you have explored in this chapter are that everyone experiences resistance, be it through thoughts, feelings, sensations or behaviours – but that you can learn to identify where you are accepting or resisting in life. You can learn to step forward towards your values in the critical moments and behave in a way that makes you fulfilled regardless of the outcome.

You have learned that thoughts are not always truths. That you do not always have to be a positive thinker. Yes, it helps but you can also accept neutral and negative thoughts and move forward too.

You do not always have to identify yourself with your thoughts, experiences or judgements. You can, through mindful awareness, step into the present moment on a consistent basis. You can move away from the autopilot experiences or habits that bring resistance. You can meet the present moment using your five senses – as though you are experiencing this moment for the first time.

When you are in the present, you can take the committed action that moves you forward. This will enable you to live from an intentional values-based perspective that makes life as fulfilling as possible for you.

CONCLUSION

IN THIS BOOK, YOU HAVE DIGESTED A LOT OF NEW mindset matches to improve your performance on and off the pitch. You have an idea at this point which elements of your mindset are working extremely well, and which need further nourishment to help you move closer to your potential.

You now have confidence in your approach to take you forward to the next level. You are clearer on what success is for you, and how you might achieve it through a preparation- and process-focused plan. You have a better understanding of how you perceive yourself and the challenges you face, and how these impact your thinking, feelings and behaviours. You have a greater sense of who you are and what your life stands for. You have identified some of the mindset obstacles that are holding you back and you are processing how you might overcome them.

When you picked up this book, you were struggling to understand why you were not achieving success more consistently. You were unsure about what you needed to do regarding your preparation, practice and performances. You were finding that motivation was based on too many external factors that were too far in the future. You were struggling with confidence when you were not getting closer to these long-term goals.

You were feeling a lack of courage in important situations where success was close. You were feeling threatened, panicked and overwhelmed when approaching important performance situations. You were unsure why you felt like this and what you could do to change how you felt.

You were feeling frustrated that your performances in a game never matched your training performances. You were often stuck in negative thinking patterns before and during important performance situations. You did not know how to break free from these negative thoughts and feelings that were zapping your energy and attention. You thought the only way to get rid of them was to outrun them or avoid the situation entirely.

At times, you were working so hard in your preparation and training but saw little or no progress in your performances. There were times when all you could think about was what was, and what would, go wrong. Your enjoyment of your sport was dwindling. You were struggling to see anything that you were doing well.

Imagine waking up one day with a new perspective and approach.

You are thinking very clearly for the first time in ages. You can recall some of the joy, freedom and fun of playing your sport to the best of your ability. You can remember being very motivated to perform well and having very clear goals that were positive, specific and controllable. You can feel this deep focus and appreciation for the present moment and the task at hand. You accept that mistakes are part of performing too, that they are not a reflection of you.

You move quickly, sharply and excitedly to each play. You are positive in your words, body language and behaviours. You are present to the opportunities that are unfolding. You love playing the game in this play-by-play focus. You love bringing an intensity, control and confidence to everything you do. You are seeing and doing things quickly, but you are not rushed. You are picking up relevant information and making clear and composed decisions that help your performance.

You are loving and embracing each new challenge. You make quick and sharp adjustments as you play. You are feeling energised, alert and challenged by the experience. At the end of the game, you feel a deep knowing about what you did well, and you bank that self-belief. You do not take positive or negative feedback personally and see it as constructive, enabling you to grow even further. You can't wait for the next session to build on the progress and express your potential even more.

I was a person and player who, at times, fell out of love with the game. I lost confidence in my ability to perform. I couldn't recognise anything I did well. I couldn't see any progress in my performances. I worried constantly about my form, what my coaches and teammates thought of me. I worried about the build-up to training, mistakes in training and failing in front of others. I was harsh and critical towards myself far too often. I was knocking my own confidence and self-belief at every available moment. Even when I did something good, I was waiting for the next mistake to happen to berate myself. I was doing extra training from a place of fear and punishment, rather than love and enjoyment. The closer I got to important performance situations, the more I worried about what could go wrong. I took all the enjoyment away from sport by having this negative, pessimistic and outcome-focused outlook.

Thankfully, by using the practices I have outlined in this book, I found a healthier and more optimistic approach to sport and life.

I began to recognise that I had more control over my mind than I realised. I began to focus on more positive aspects of myself. I began to understand who I was and what I stood for. I began to know my deeper motives for playing the game. I began to focus on my process rather than results. I began to enjoy my relationships, training and games much more. I began to recognise the other areas I contributed to as a father, husband, son, brother and friend. I began to care less about what others thought of me. I had a better idea and approach to what success, health and happiness were for me. I began to recognise and appreciate all I had in my life and look forward with optimism to what could be achieved.

Through my experiences in life, I have learned to understand that it is about the journey, not the destination.

Very often you might think that success at the end of the year will bring you the happiness or joy you are craving – but it is the experiences along the way that hold that joy, growth and happiness. The more positive, present and appreciative of these experiences you are, the better you will feel, and the better your life will be.

You begin to enjoy the learning, growth and skills you develop from challenges. You have the power to choose to focus on what went well, what you enjoy and what you are grateful for having. Yes, there will always be things you can develop and be better at, but you are not limited by these things. No one on this planet is perfect at everything. There is no game in which every player has a perfect performance every time and never makes mistakes.

In team sport, only one team can win. Does that make every other team a failure?

In individual sport, only one person can win a tournament. Does that make all the other competitors failures?

You have the power to decide this but be conscious of your interpretation of success and failure. It can alter your motivation, effort and performances in the future. That is why having clarity about what success is for you – why it matters, who you want to be – and focusing on mastery of your process and tasks over outcomes, appraising situations as challenges rather than threats, practising an optimistic approach and building psychological flexibility are important skills to keep coming back to. They will help you to not get caught up in others' expectations of success for you. They will help you to reduce the need for outside validation. They will help you to experience more joy, love and gratitude for your everyday experiences.

My wish for you in life is to experience your sport and life in a way that makes it enjoyable, motivating and fulfilling. That your sport is something you do for enjoyment and development. That you realise it is something you play, not who you are. That it is an opportunity for you to develop your personality on and off the field. That it enables you to develop your values, your communication skills, your competence and confidence, to connect with others and share many positive learning experiences with them.

Through having challenges in life and reflecting on them accurately, you can develop your resources to cope. Sport will present varied and difficult challenges for you. Without stretching and challenging yourself in life, you can begin to stagnate mentally, emotionally and physically. By having goals and ambitions to pursue, you begin to access more of what you're capable of. By focusing on why you want to succeed and how, you begin to develop in new and exciting ways.

Building consistent healthy habits and routines will not only improve your sport performance but will also have huge benefits in terms of your health, well-being and relationships. Being able to approach important situations with excitement rather than fear will enable you to access even more of your skills and qualities, to continue to reach new levels of performance on and off the field. Having the ability to access high self-confidence, having a high level of self-control over your mind and body, and approaching each moment with a positive focus on the task at hand will enable you to be a consistent performer and to excel in pressure moments. Having the awareness and behaviours in place to move towards your values will cultivate greater joy, happiness and fulfilment in all aspects of your life.

ACKNOWLEDGEMENTS

I have been fortunate in my life to be a part of a great community in Boleybeg, Rahoon, a wonderful club, and many amazing teams in sport and business. I would like to thank the following team of people who played a part in guiding me on the journey and helping me in putting my experiences together on paper in *MVP*.

To my publishers Hachette Books Ireland, in particular Ciara Doorley who patiently helped me put the book together piece by piece with the help of Stephen Riordan and Claire Rourke. To Joanna and Elaine in marketing and publicity and Ellie in helping with the audiobook.

To my writing coach Elaine O'Neill, who assisted me to begin the journey and helped me to secure the publishing contract, your expertise, support and encouragement were invaluable.

To my best men Robert, Gerry, Damien and Paul. To my closest friends Tomo, Gooch, Boggy, Motty, Shaneo, Sean, JP,

Podsi, Brian, MJ, Chunky, Lynchy, Darragh and Pat, thank you for all the fun times and support down the years; I look forward to many more laughs along the way.

To my many mentors whose loyalty, advice and support I value so much. Thank you, Mam and Dad, Gerry Hussey, Robert Keane, John and Martin Kearns, Fran O'Reilly, Austin Sammon, Eamon O'Shea, Conor Hayes and Seán Silke.

To my many teammates, coaches, managers and backroom staff from underage up to senior, from schools, colleges, club and county, thank you for your guidance, support and friendship throughout the journey so far.

To the many individuals, teams and organisations I have been fortunate to meet and work for over the last ten years, thank you so much for your trust, belief and openness to exploring high performance practices with me. I am forever grateful for the opportunities I have been given.

To my family in Boleybeg, I count myself very fortunate where I grew up and the wonderful support I have got from my parents, sisters, neighbours – in particular the Keanes, Coynes and Nallys – friends and my club Rahoon/Newcastle. You helped me become the person I am today, and to realise some of my biggest dreams in life and share those memories with you has been extra special. I will be eternally grateful to you all.

To my neighbours in Athenry who have made us so welcome as a family, especially the Byrnes, Crawfords, Joyces, Darren and Fiona and the Trotters.

To the dawn bombers for your wonderful support down the years.

To Harry, Margaret and the Bauld Barretts, thank you for your unwavering love and support, and I look forward to many fun years ahead with you on this exciting journey we are on.

BIBLIOGRAPHY

Bandura, A., *Self-Efficacy: The Exercise of Control*. 1997. W. H. Freeman.

Blascovich, J. 'Challenge and Threat.' In A. J. Elliot (ed.), *Handbook of Approach and Avoidance Motivation* (pp. 431–445). 2018. Psychology Press.

Brimmell, J., Parker, J. K., Wilson, M. R. and Vine, S. J., 'Challenge and Threat States, Performance, and Attentional Control During a Pressurized Soccer Penalty Task'. *Sport, Exercise, and Performance Psychology*. 8(1). 2018.

Csikszentmihalyi, M., *Flow: The Psychology of Optimal Experience*. 1989. Harper and Row.

Elliot, A. J. and McGregor, H. A., 'A 2 × 2 Achievement Goal Framework.' *Journal of Personality and Social Psychology*. 80(3). 2001.

Forlenza, S. T., Vealey, R. and Mackersie, J., 'Coaching Behaviours that Enhance Confidence in Athletes and Teams'. *International Sport Coaching Journal*. 5(3). 2018.

Gallway, T., *The Inner Game of Golf*. 2009. Random House.

Kotler, S., *The Rise of Superman*. 2014. Amazon Publishing.

Kübler-Ross, E., *On Death and Dying: What the Dying Have to Teach Doctors, Nurses, Clergy and Their Own Families*. 2014. Scribner.

McCaw, R., *The Real McCaw: The Autobiography*. 2015. Aurum.

Meijen, C., Turner, M., Jones, M. V., Sheffield, D. and McCarthy, P., 'A Theory of Challenge and Threat States in Athletes: A Revised Conceptualization'. *Frontiers in Psychology*. 11(126). 2020.

Mercer, J., 'River of Life Exercise'. https://onbeing.org/wp-content/uploads/2019/05/on-being-river-of-life-exercise.pdf

Newman, M. *Emotional Capitalists: The New Leaders*. 2008. John Wiley & Sons.

Porges, S. W., *The Polyvagal Theory: Neurophysiological Foundations of Emotions, Attachment, Communication, and Self-regulation*. 2011. W. W. Norton.

Rachman, S. J., *Fear and Courage* (2nd ed.). 1990. W. H. Freeman and Company.

Rotella, B., *Your 15th Club: The Inner Secret to Great Golf*. 2008. Free Pass.

Seligman, M., *Learned Optimism: How to Change Your Mind and Your Life*. 2006. Vintage.

Warrell, Margie, 'Do You Know Your "Why?" 4 Questions To Find Your Purpose'. 2014. *Forbes*. www.forbes.com/sites/margiewarrell/2013/10/30/know-your-why-4-questions-to-tap-the-power-of-purpose/

Yerkes, R. M. and Dodson, J. D., 'The Relation of Strength of Stimulus to Rapidity of Habit-Formation'. *Journal of Comparative Neurology and Psychology*. 18. 1908.